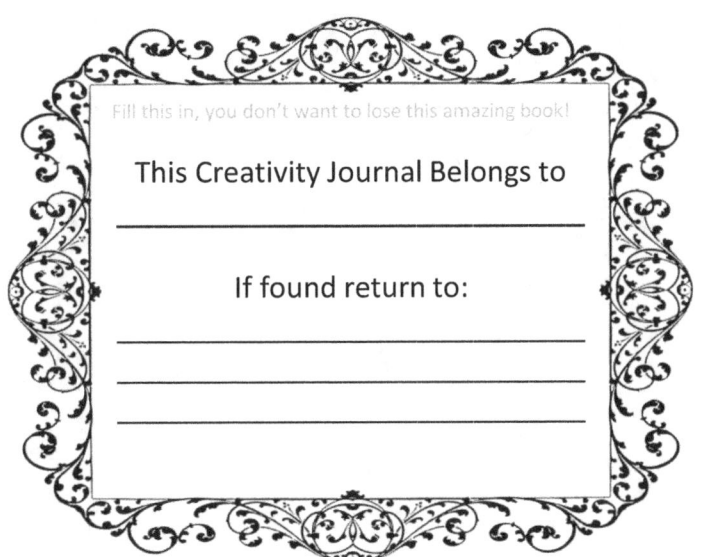

Fill this in, you don't want to lose this amazing book!

This Creativity Journal Belongs to
_____

If found return to:
_____
_____
_____

My Creativity Journal

Draw a picture of yourself: so people know who owns this book. Don't worry if you can't draw.

I added a shape to get you started 😊

© 2020 by Larissa Russell of Creative U

All Rights Reserved. No part of this publication may be reproduced, distributed, or transmitted in any form or by any means, including photocopying, recording, or other electronic or mechanical methods, without prior written permission of the publisher, except in the case of brief quotations embodied in critical reviews and certain other non-commercial uses permitted by copyright law. For permission requests write to the publisher addressed "Attention: Permissions Coordinator," at the address below.

ISBN: 9781679686443

Front cover image courtesy of pixabay.com
Design by Larissa Russell
Images provided by pixabay.com

Printed by Kindle Direct Publishing

First printing edition 2020.

Creative U Publishing
10308 114 St , Suite 301
Edmonton, AB T5K 2X2
Canada

www.CreativeU.ca

After I created my 'Have an Amazingly Creative Day Journal' many people said they needed more information, more prompts. They weren't sure where to start. So this journal was born from all that amazing feedback.

I hope you enjoy it as much as they do.
Have an Amazingly Creative Day,

Larissa

YOU TOO CAN HAVE AN AMAZINGLY CREATIVE DAY!

Let's start our
Daily Creative Practice.
Wait, what?
How do we do that?
Fill in the blanks everywhere and
have fun doing it!
That's it.

This book has everything you need to start your creative day.
- ✹ Morning Habits
- ✹ Journaling
- ✹ Today's Creative Pursuit
- ✹ Affirmations
- ✹ Doodling
- ✹ Notes
- ✹ Coloring

Do as little or as much as you want each day, adding a little something each day will help you create your daily creative practice.
They say it takes 21 days to establish a habit.
Try at least 21 days in a row and see how you feel.

Color everything in this book, add more to the picture. Use your creativity.

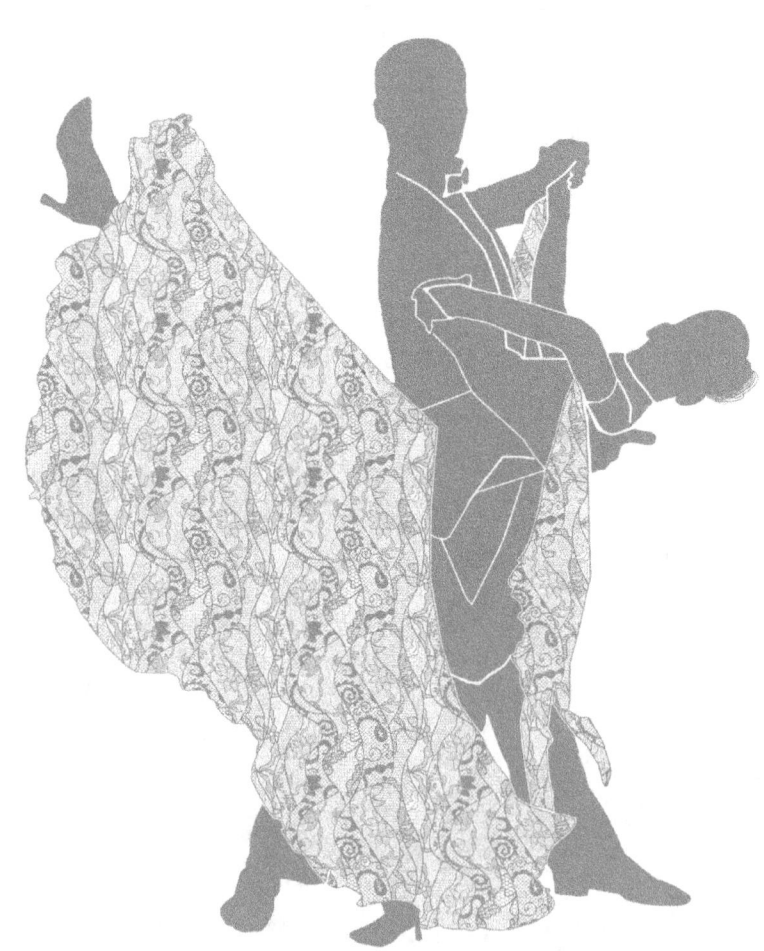

What is Creativity?

We often think about creativity as making something "Artistic", but in fact the root meaning of the word means 'to grow'. Creativity's by-products are some of the major achievements of civilization - from the invention of the wheel to our amazing technology we use today.

We are all creative individuals, but sometimes we don't feel like we are. If we can build our creative muscles, it can help in so may areas of our lives. Creativity helps with our mental health, our careers, it makes life more interesting and fulfilling.

Many people don't identify as creative and believe they won't be able to make art. The special surprise is that everyone is creative. No artistic talent is needed to participate in creative healing or to do creative activities on your own.

Why we Create.

When we create something it moves from the internal (an idea) to the external (the expression).

- We express thoughts and emotions that can be hard to put into words
- We lower stress and anxiety
- We relax and feel calmer and happier
- We connect with ourselves on a deep level, no matter what we are going through
- We find meaning in life experiences
- We find new ways to cope with grief and loss
- We form new connections with others
- We shift our focus away from pain or stressful thoughts to activities that are soothing, enjoyable and fun
- We create something unique that gives us a sense of pleasure and accomplishment

Each day there is space for you to track your morning habits, set your affirmations for the day, journal, add in today's creative pursuits and space to color, doodle and make notes.

There are no rules for this book. I challenge you to start a creative practice by doing something everyday, but if you don't that is ok too. Just show up when you can. Have fun, and let yourself explore and create.

Take a look at the next page and it will give you more details about the daily pages. If you ever have any questions feel free to contact Larissa at;
Larissa@CreativeU.ca
or stop by the website and see what else is going on and ask your questions there www.CreativeU.ca
You can also find Creative U on Facebook www.facebook.com/CreativeU.ca or Instagram www.Instagram.com/CreativeU.ca

Coloring – The pictures used in this journal have been chosen to spark creativity, some may seem odd, some may seem weird, some may even make you wonder how on earth you are going to color that picture. That's the fun part, there are no rules here. You can color or not, maybe you will have a purple penguin, maybe a blue elephant, it's all up to you. You will also find that the pictures are in tones of grey. This has been done to give free rein to change the pictures, make them something else. Use them as a jumping off point for your creativity. Use them however fits you best. If you want to color, do that, if you want to make them into something else do that, if you want to make them a small piece of larger picture do that, maybe you want to ignore the picture and create your own. Whatever you want to do is the right thing, this is your creativity journal.

The most important part is to enjoy the experience.

You recreate yourself, when you relax.
- Lailah Gifty Akita

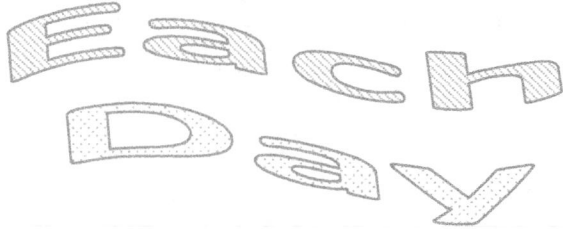

Each Day

Morning Habits – What are your morning habits;
- What time do I get up to accomplish these morning tasks?
- How many glasses of water will I drink today?
- How many minutes of meditation Did I do?
- Have I journaled today?
- What else do I want to accomplish this morning?

Check off each one that you accomplish each day.

Meditation – Each day sit in stillness and listen to your breathing in… and out. Increase your meditation by one minute a week until you can sit in stillness for 15 min a day.

A Journaling page is included each day. If you are able to do more, add a notebook to continue writing. Sometimes it may feel like you have nothing to say, but just write '*I have nothing to say*' until it comes, and inevitably it will start to flow. Just keep writing. You can use the quote to prompt you or you can write whatever moves you.

You will find **Coloring/Note pages** each day. You can jot notes, color, make a grocery list, whatever you need this page for. I love it to jot down all my amazingly creative ideas that come out after I finish journaling.

Today's Creative Pursuit – What are your plans today to bring your creativity out to play? Maybe you will be decorating cookies, or working on a video of your kids or grand kids. Maybe you are designing your garden, or making a gift for a friend. What is your creative pursuit for today?

Today's Affirmations – What positive statements are you going to tell yourself today?
1. Keep it positive
2. Use present tense
3. Make it about you

Examples: "I am creating with reckless abandon today and am excited to see what shows up" Or "I am spending time in pursuits that make me happy". Now repeat it to yourself at least 3 times through out the day.

Doodle boxes are there for your fun each day, you will also find fun drawings for coloring all through out the pages. Use them to color and even add more creativity to them, fill in the page. Break out the colored pencils, markers, crayons or even the paint to fill in the pages.

The benefits of coloring. I have added a lot of coloring prompts through out the journal. It helps relieve stress. It's like a mindful meditation. Spend 10 minutes a day coloring and you will notice the difference. Feeling overwhelmed and unproductive? Take 10 minutes for yourself, break out the crayons, pencil crayons or markers and color away your stress.

Date _____

> The creative adult is the child who survived.
> - Ursula Leguin

MORNING HABITS

What are the habits I want to build, increase or pay attention to? Sleep, water, meditation and journaling are the ones that are high on my list, what else do you want to add?

- [ ] 1. My time to get up is _____ am.
- [ ] 2. I will drink _____ glasses of water.
- [ ] 3. I did _____ minutes of Meditation.
- [ ] 4. I Journaled this morning.
- [ ] 5. _____
- [ ] 6. _____

Today's Creative Pursuit

What creativity will I pursue today? Baking, decorating, coloring, painting, music, creating software or a spreadsheet? The possibilities are endless.

_____
_____
_____

Today's Affirmations

Today's affirmations? I am creative, I am pursuing my dreams today, I am open to possibilities. What positive, present, personal statement are you making for yourself today? Repeat it at least 3 times today.

_____
_____
_____

One action I will take today to make myself or my life better.

Today I will try a new food, today I will go to the gym, today I will send that application, the possibilities are endless. What will you do today to make you life better?

_____
_____

One thing I will do today that is slightly out of my comfort zone.

Those scary things that you think you can't do. What is the worst that will happen? Make that phone call, ask for that raise, create that video, do what ever it takes to pull yourself out of your comfort zone, just one small thing each day will make a huge difference.

_____
_____

Doodle of the Day

I'm experimental by nature... always exploring my creativity. -Christina Aguilera

How does this quote make you feel?

Notes

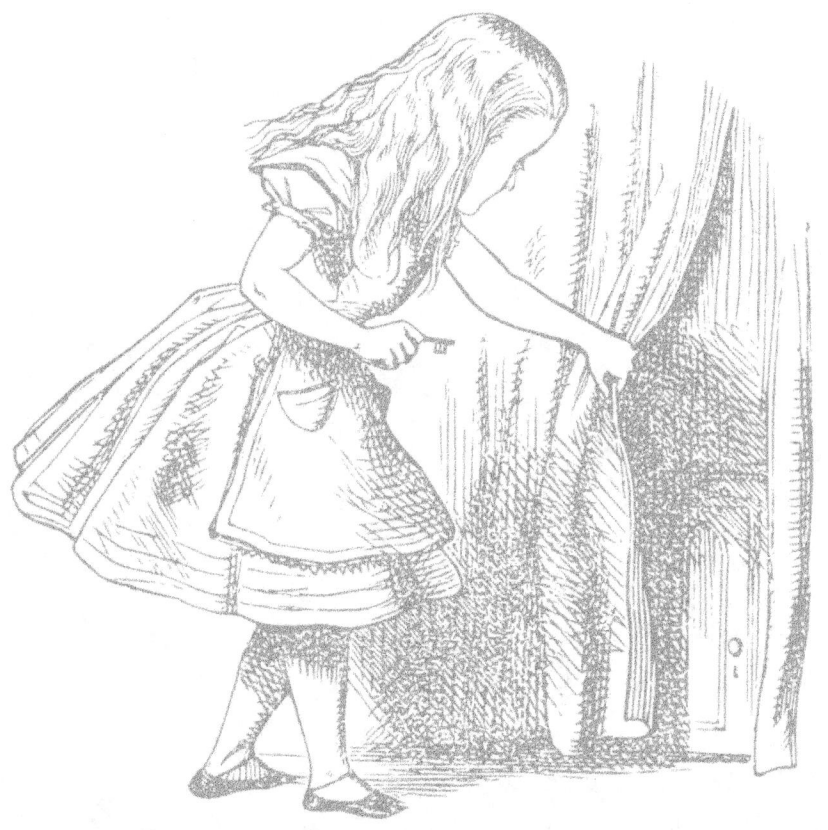

Date _____

> Curiosity about life in all of its aspects, I think, is still the secret of great creative people. -Leo Burnett

Today's Creative Pursuit

What creativity will I pursue today? Baking, decorating, coloring, painting, music, creating software or a spreadsheet? The possibilities are endless.

_____
_____
_____

MORNING HABITS

What are the habits I want to build, increase or pay attention to? Sleep, water, meditation and journaling are the ones that are high on my list, what else do you want to add?

- [ ] 1. My time to get up is _____ am.
- [ ] 2. I will drink _____ glasses of water.
- [ ] 3. I did _____ minutes of Meditation.
- [ ] 4. I Journaled this morning.
- [ ] 5. _____
- [ ] 6. _____

Today's Affirmations

Today's affirmations? I am creative, I am pursuing my dreams today, I am open to possibilities. What positive, present, personal statement are you making for yourself today? Repeat it at least 3 times today.

_____
_____
_____

One action I will take today to make myself or my life better.

Today I will try a new food, today I will go to the gym, today I will send that application, the possibilities are endless. What will you do today to make you life better?

_____
_____

One thing I will do today that is slightly out of my comfort zone.

Those scary things that you think you can't do. What is the worst that will happen? Make that phone call, ask for that raise, create that video, do what ever it takes to pull yourself out of your comfort zone, just one small thing each day will make a huge difference.

_____
_____

Doodle of the Day

Our creative dreams and yearnings come from a divine source. -Julia Cameron

How does this quote make you feel?

Notes

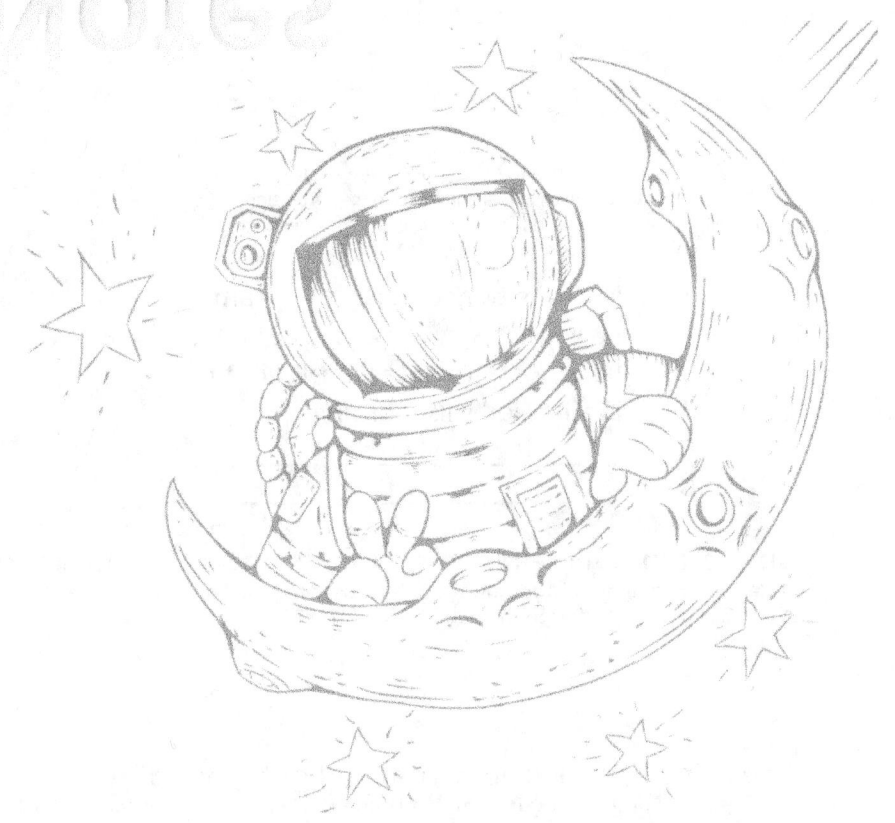

Date _____

> Learn the rules like a pro, so you can break them like an artist.
> -Pablo Picasso

Today's Creative Pursuit

What creativity will I pursue today? Baking, decorating, coloring, painting, music, creating software or a spreadsheet? The possibilities are endless.

_____
_____
_____

MORNING HABITS

What are the habits I want to build, increase or pay attention to? Sleep, water, meditation and journaling are the ones that are high on my list, what else do you want to add?

- [ ] 1. My time to get up is _____ am.
- [ ] 2. I will drink _____ glasses of water.
- [ ] 3. I did _____ minutes of Meditation.
- [ ] 4. I Journaled this morning.
- [ ] 5. _____
- [ ] 6. _____

Today's Affirmations

Today's affirmations? I am creative, I am pursuing my dreams today, I am open to possibilities. What positive, present, personal statement are you making for yourself today? Repeat it at least 3 times today.

_____
_____
_____

One action I will take today to make myself or my life better.
Today I will try a new food, today I will go to the gym, today I will send that application, the possibilities are endless. What will you do today to make you life better?

_____
_____

One thing I will do today that is slightly out of my comfort zone.
Those scary things that you think you can't do. What is the worst that will happen? Make that phone call, ask for that raise, create that video, do what ever it takes to pull yourself out of your comfort zone, just one small thing each day will make a huge difference.

_____

Doodle of the Day

Truly creative people care a little about what they have done, and a lot about what they are doing. -Alan Cohen

How does this quote make you feel?

Notes

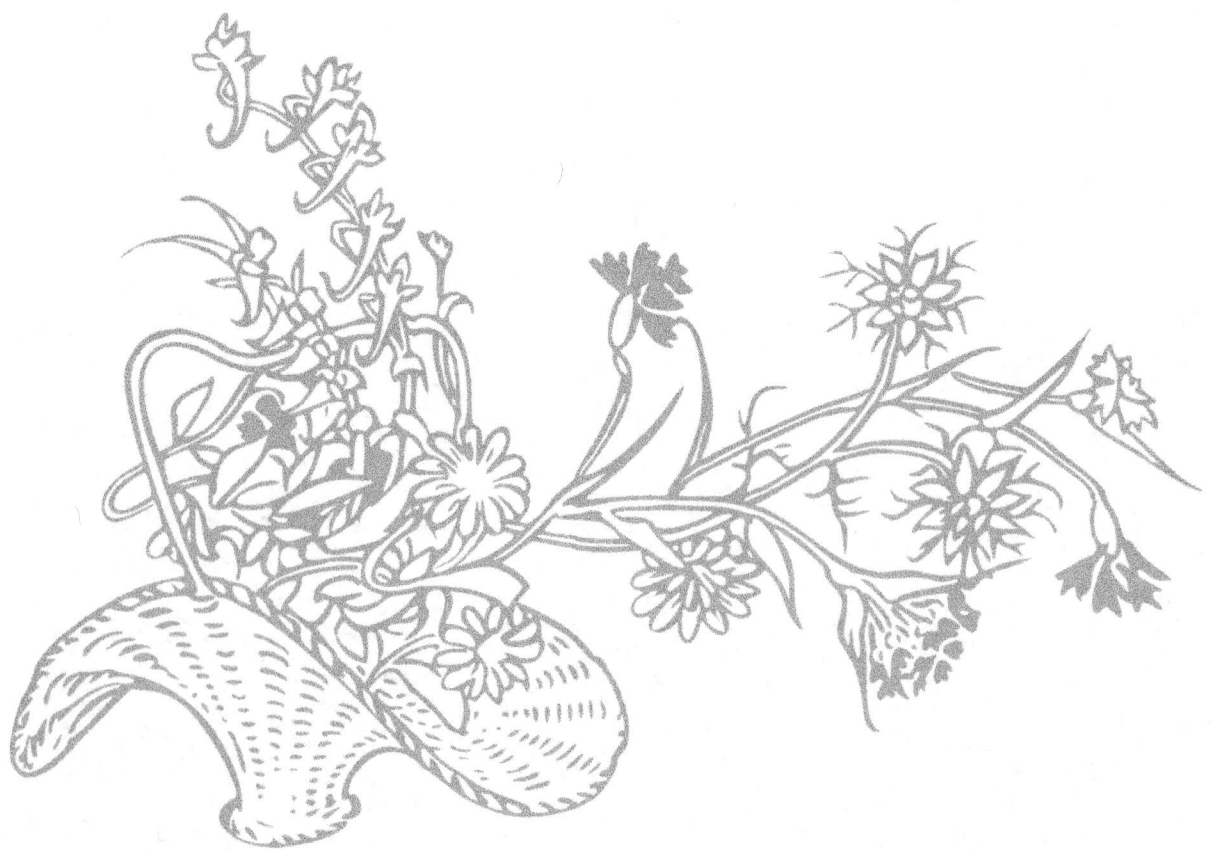

Date _____

An idea that is not dangerous is unworthy of being called an idea at all. -Oscar Wilde

MORNING HABITS

What are the habits I want to build, increase or pay attention to? Sleep, water, meditation and journaling are the ones that are high on my list, what else do you want to add?

☐ 1. My time to get up is _____ am.
☐ 2. I will drink _____ glasses of water.
☐ 3. I did _____ minutes of Meditation.
☐ 4. I Journaled this morning.
☐ 5. _____
☐ 6. _____

Today's Creative Pursuit

What creativity will I pursue today? Baking, decorating, coloring, painting, music, creating software or a spreadsheet? The possibilities are endless.

_____

_____

_____

Today's Affirmations

Today's affirmations? I am creative, I am pursuing my dreams today, I am open to possibilities. What positive, present, personal statement are you making for yourself today? Repeat it at least 3 times today.

_____

_____

_____

One action I will take today to make myself or my life better.

Today I will try a new food, today I will go to the gym, today I will send that application, the possibilities are endless. What will you do today to make you life better?

_____

_____

One thing I will do today that is slightly out of my comfort zone.

Those scary things that you think you can't do. What is the worst that will happen? Make that phone call, ask for that raise, create that video, do what ever it takes to pull yourself out of your comfort zone, just one small thing each day will make a huge difference.

_____

Doodle of the Day

If you're alive, you're a creative person. -Elizabeth Gilbert

How does this quote make you feel?

Notes

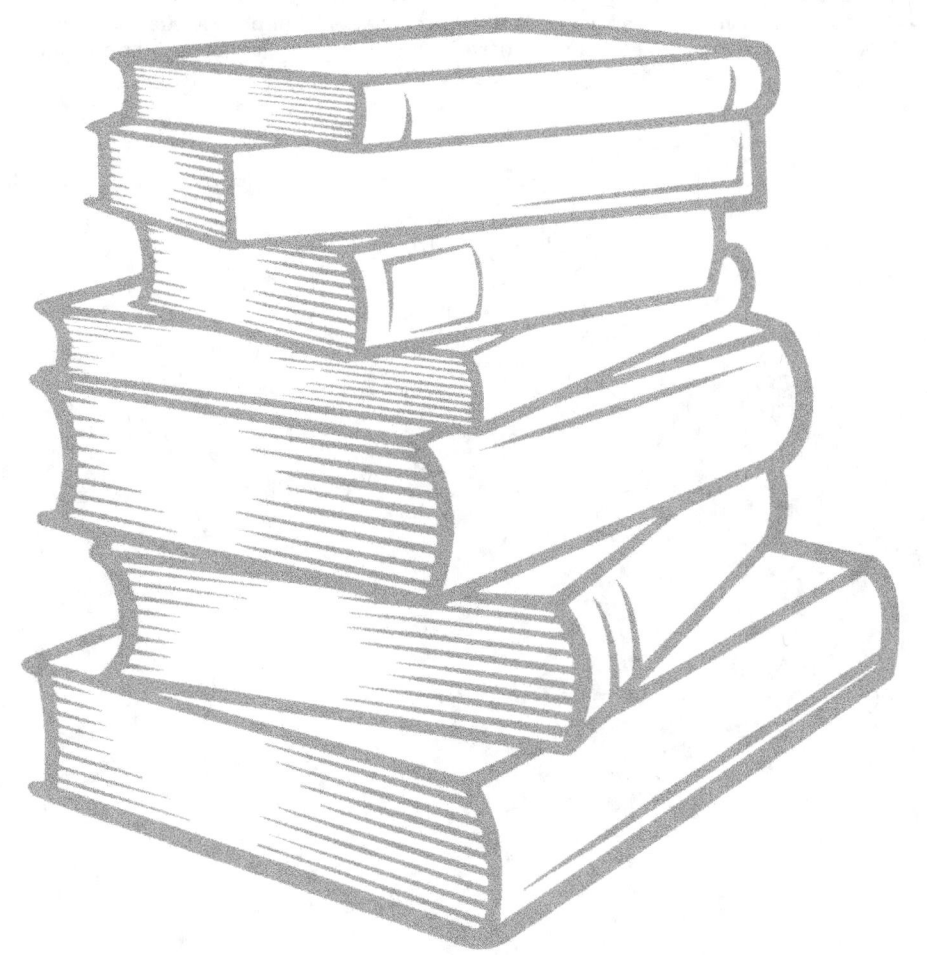

Date _____

> It's not where you take things from – it's where you take them to.
> -Jean-Luc Godard

MORNING HABITS

What are the habits I want to build, increase or pay attention to? Sleep, water, meditation and journaling are the ones that are high on my list, what else do you want to add?

- [ ] 1. My time to get up is _____ am.
- [ ] 2. I will drink _____ glasses of water.
- [ ] 3. I did _____ minutes of Meditation.
- [ ] 4. I Journaled this morning.
- [ ] 5. _____
- [ ] 6. _____

Today's Creative Pursuit

What creativity will I pursue today? Baking, decorating, coloring, painting, music, creating software or a spreadsheet? The possibilities are endless.

_____
_____

Today's Affirmations

Today's affirmations? I am creative, I am pursuing my dreams today, I am open to possibilities. What positive, present, personal statement are you making for yourself today? Repeat it at least 3 times today.

_____
_____
_____

One action I will take today to make myself or my life better.

Today I will try a new food, today I will go to the gym, today I will send that application, the possibilities are endless. What will you do today to make you life better?

_____
_____

One thing I will do today that is slightly out of my comfort zone.

Those scary things that you think you can't do. What is the worst that will happen? Make that phone call, ask for that raise, create that video, do what ever it takes to pull yourself out of your comfort zone, just one small thing each day will make a huge difference.

_____
_____

Doodle of the Day

A truly creative person rids him or herself of all self-imposed limitations. - Gerald G. Jampolsky

How does this quote make you feel?

Notes

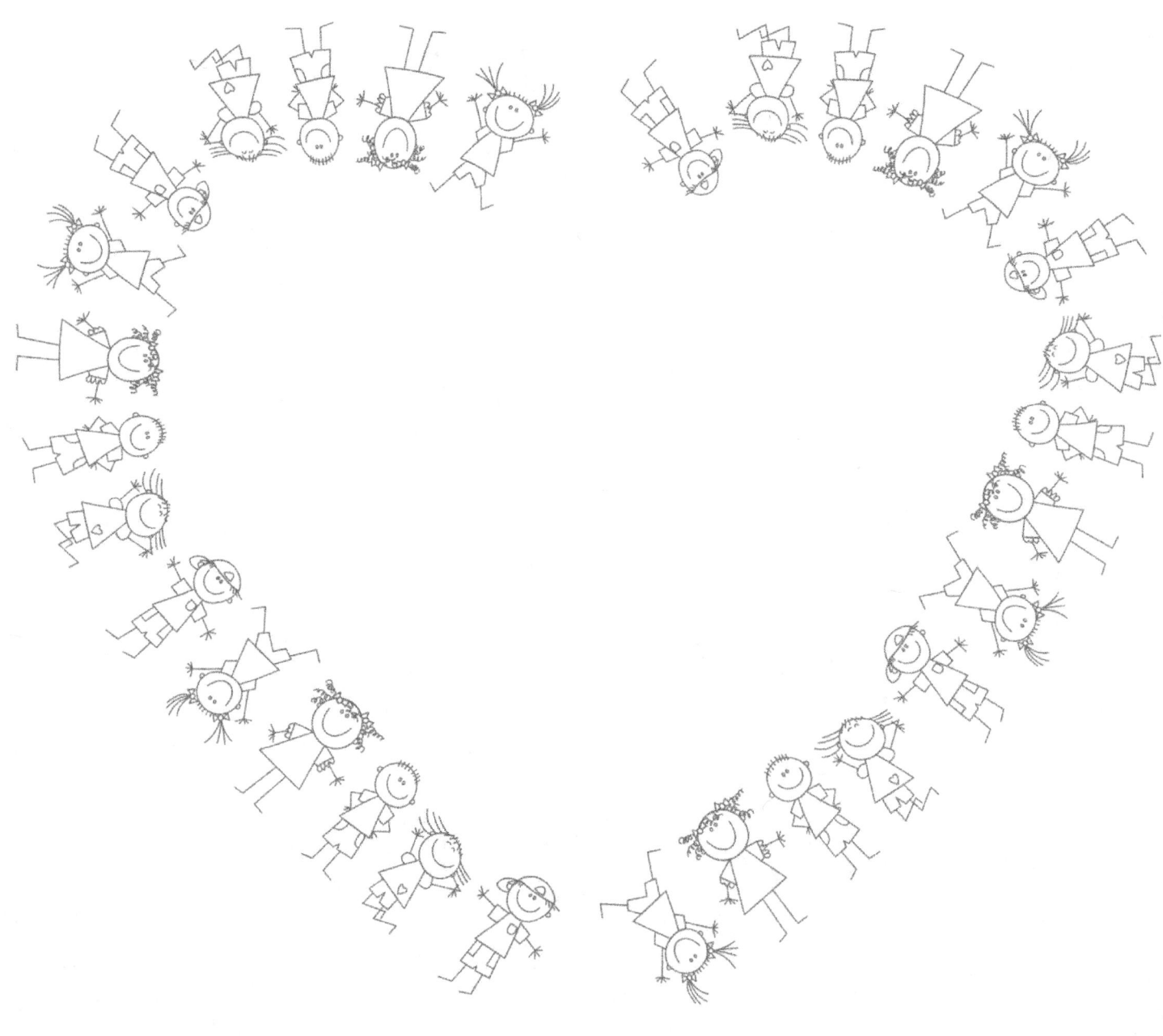

Date _____

> The difficulty lies not so much in developing new ideas as in escaping from old ones. -John Maynard Keynes

MORNING HABITS

What are the habits I want to build, increase or pay attention to? Sleep, water, meditation and journaling are the ones that are high on my list, what else do you want to add?

- ☐ 1. My time to get up is _____ am.
- ☐ 2. I will drink _____ glasses of water.
- ☐ 3. I did _____ minutes of Meditation.
- ☐ 4. I Journaled this morning.
- ☐ 5. _____
- ☐ 6. _____

Today's Creative Pursuit

What creativity will I pursue today? Baking, decorating, coloring, painting, music, creating software or a spreadsheet? The possibilities are endless.

_____
_____
_____

Today's Affirmations

Today's affirmations? I am creative, I am pursuing my dreams today, I am open to possibilities. What positive, present, personal statement are you making for yourself today? Repeat it at least 3 times today.

_____
_____
_____

One action I will take today to make myself or my life better.

Today I will try a new food, today I will go to the gym, today I will send that application, the possibilities are endless. What will you do today to make you life better?

_____
_____

One thing I will do today that is slightly out of my comfort zone.

Those scary things that you think you can't do. What is the worst that will happen? Make that phone call, ask for that raise, create that video, do what ever it takes to pull yourself out of your comfort zone, just one small thing each day will make a huge difference.

_____
_____

Doodle of the Day

Life is trying things to see if they work. -Ray Bradbury

How does this quote make you feel?

Notes

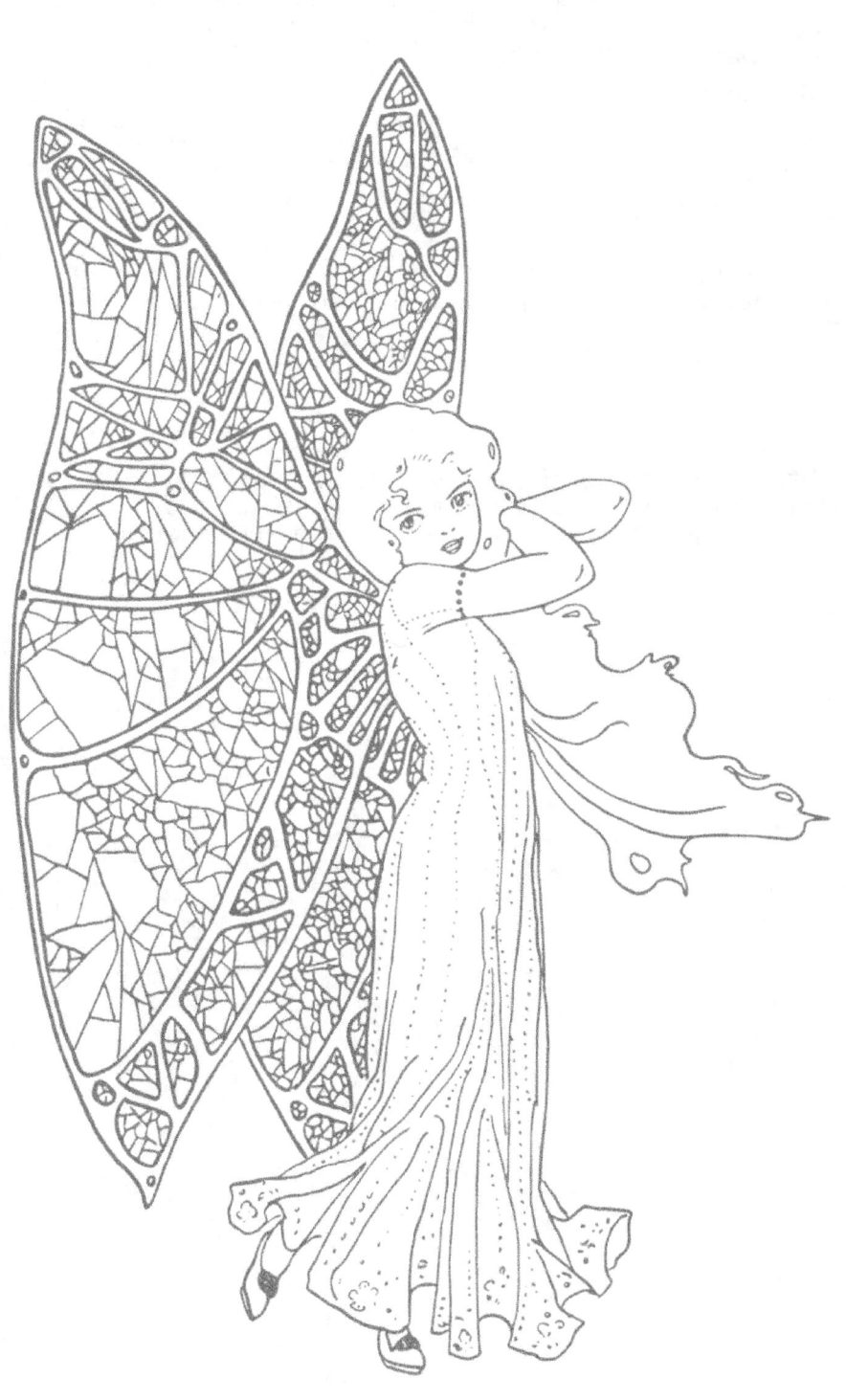

Date _____

> To live a creative life, we must lose our fear of being wrong.
> -Joseph Chilton Pierce

MORNING HABITS

What are the habits I want to build, increase or pay attention to? Sleep, water, meditation and journaling are the ones that are high on my list, what else do you want to add?

- [ ] 1. My time to get up is _____ am.
- [ ] 2. I will drink _____ glasses of water.
- [ ] 3. I did _____ minutes of Meditation.
- [ ] 4. I Journaled this morning.
- [ ] 5. _____
- [ ] 6. _____

Today's Creative Pursuit

What creativity will I pursue today? Baking, decorating, coloring, painting, music, creating software or a spreadsheet? The possibilities are endless.

_____
_____

Today's Affirmations

Today's affirmations? I am creative, I am pursuing my dreams today, I am open to possibilities. What positive, present, personal statement are you making for yourself today? Repeat it at least 3 times today.

_____
_____

One action I will take today to make myself or my life better.

Today I will try a new food, today I will go to the gym, today I will send that application, the possibilities are endless. What will you do today to make you life better?

_____
_____

One thing I will do today that is slightly out of my comfort zone.

Those scary things that you think you can't do. What is the worst that will happen? Make that phone call, ask for that raise, create that video, do what ever it takes to pull yourself out of your comfort zone, just one small thing each day will make a huge difference.

_____

Doodle of the Day

Do not fear to be eccentric in opinion, for every opinion now accepted was once eccentric. -Bertrand Russell

How does this quote make you feel?

Notes

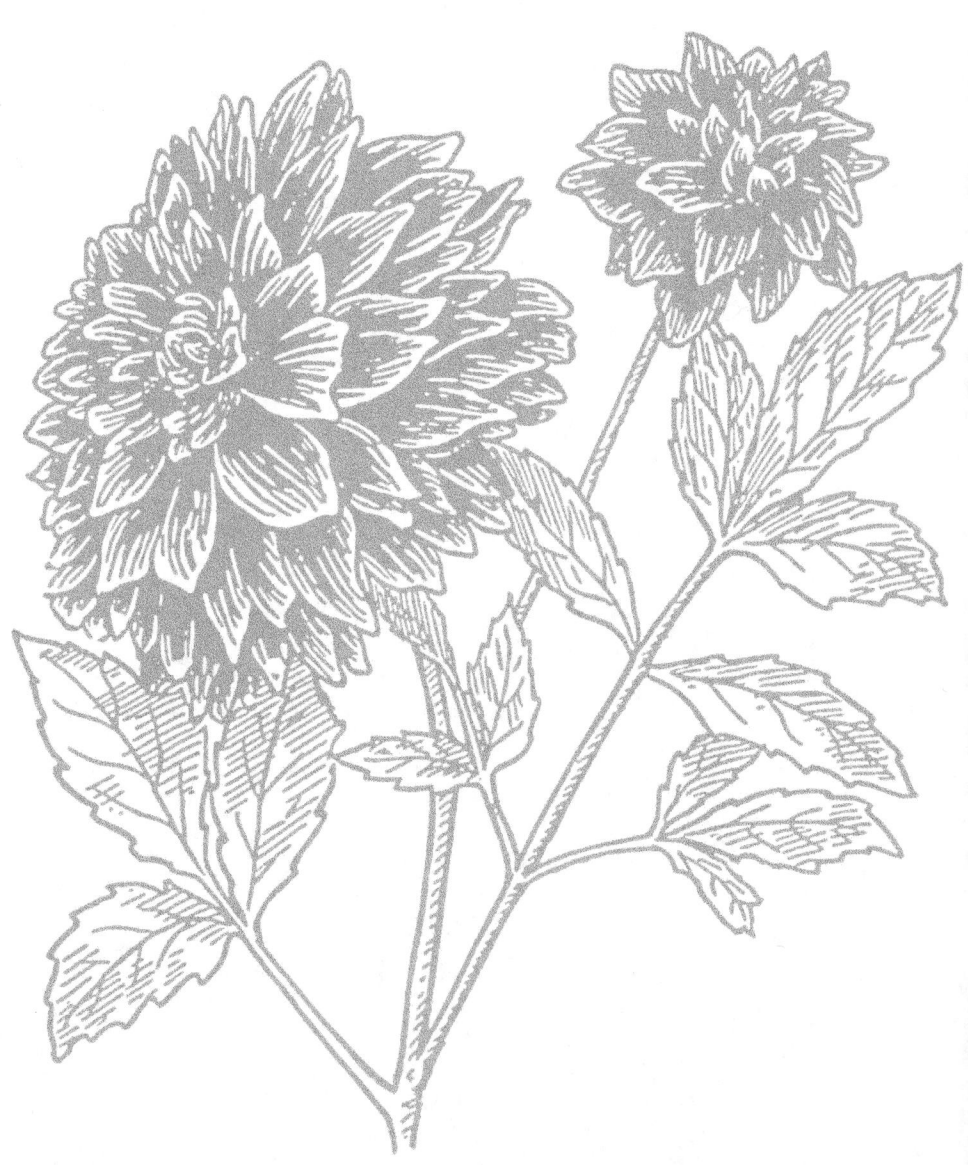

Date _____

> An idea that is developed and put into action is more important than an idea that exists only as an idea.
> -Edward de Bono

Today's Creative Pursuit

What creativity will I pursue today? Baking, decorating, coloring, painting, music, creating software or a spreadsheet? The possibilities are endless.

_____

_____

_____

MORNING HABITS

What are the habits I want to build, increase or pay attention to? Sleep, water, meditation and journaling are the ones that are high on my list, what else do you want to add?

- ☐ 1. My time to get up is _____ am.
- ☐ 2. I will drink _____ glasses of water.
- ☐ 3. I did _____ minutes of Meditation.
- ☐ 4. I Journaled this morning.
- ☐ 5. _____
- ☐ 6. _____

Today's Affirmations

Today's affirmations? I am creative, I am pursuing my dreams today, I am open to possibilities. What positive, present, personal statement are you making for yourself today? Repeat it at least 3 times today.

_____

_____

_____

One action I will take today to make myself or my life better.

Today I will try a new food, today I will go to the gym, today I will send that application, the possibilities are endless. What will you do today to make you life better?

_____

_____

One thing I will do today that is slightly out of my comfort zone.

Those scary things that you think you can't do. What is the worst that will happen? Make that phone call, ask for that raise, create that video, do what ever it takes to pull yourself out of your comfort zone, just one small thing each day will make a huge difference.

_____

_____

Doodle of the Day

You can't wait for inspiration; you have to go after it with a club. -Jack London

How does this quote make you feel?

Notes

Date _____

> A man may die, nations may rise and fall,
> but an idea lives on.
> -John F. Kennedy

MORNING HABITS

What are the habits I want to build, increase or pay attention to? Sleep, water, meditation and journaling are the ones that are high on my list, what else do you want to add?

- ☐ 1. My time to get up is _____ am.
- ☐ 2. I will drink _____ glasses of water.
- ☐ 3. I did _____ minutes of Meditation.
- ☐ 4. I Journaled this morning.
- ☐ 5. _____
- ☐ 6. _____

Today's Creative Pursuit

What creativity will I pursue today? Baking, decorating, coloring, painting, music, creating software or a spreadsheet? The possibilities are endless.

_____
_____
_____

Today's Affirmations

Today's affirmations? I am creative, I am pursuing my dreams today, I am open to possibilities. What positive, present, personal statement are you making for yourself today? Repeat it at least 3 times today.

_____
_____
_____

One action I will take today to make myself or my life better.

Today I will try a new food, today I will go to the gym, today I will send that application, the possibilities are endless. What will you do today to make you life better?

_____
_____

One thing I will do today that is slightly out of my comfort zone.

Those scary things that you think you can't do. What is the worst that will happen? Make that phone call, ask for that raise, create that video, do what ever it takes to pull yourself out of your comfort zone, just one small thing each day will make a huge difference.

_____

Doodle of the Day

You do not need anybody's permission to live a creative life. -Elizabeth Gilbert

How does this quote make you feel?

Notes

Date _____

> By believing passionately in something that still does not exist, we create it.
> -Nikos Kazantzakis

Today's Creative Pursuit

What creativity will I pursue today? Baking, decorating, coloring, painting, music, creating software or a spreadsheet? The possibilities are endless.

_____
_____
_____

MORNING HABITS

What are the habits I want to build, increase or pay attention to? Sleep, water, meditation and journaling are the ones that are high on my list, what else do you want to add?

- ☐ 1. My time to get up is _____ am.
- ☐ 2. I will drink _____ glasses of water.
- ☐ 3. I did _____ minutes of Meditation.
- ☐ 4. I Journaled this morning.
- ☐ 5. _____
- ☐ 6. _____

Today's Affirmations

Today's affirmations? I am creative, I am pursuing my dreams today, I am open to possibilities. What positive, present, personal statement are you making for yourself today? Repeat it at least 3 times today.

_____
_____
_____

One action I will take today to make myself or my life better.
Today I will try a new food, today I will go to the gym, today I will send that application, the possibilities are endless. What will you do today to make you life better?

_____
_____

One thing I will do today that is slightly out of my comfort zone.
Those scary things that you think you can't do. What is the worst that will happen? Make that phone call, ask for that raise, create that video, do what ever it takes to pull yourself out of your comfort zone, just one small thing each day will make a huge difference.

_____
_____

Doodle of the Day

You need chaos in your soul to give birth to a dancing star. -Friedrich Nietzsche

How does this quote make you feel?

Notes

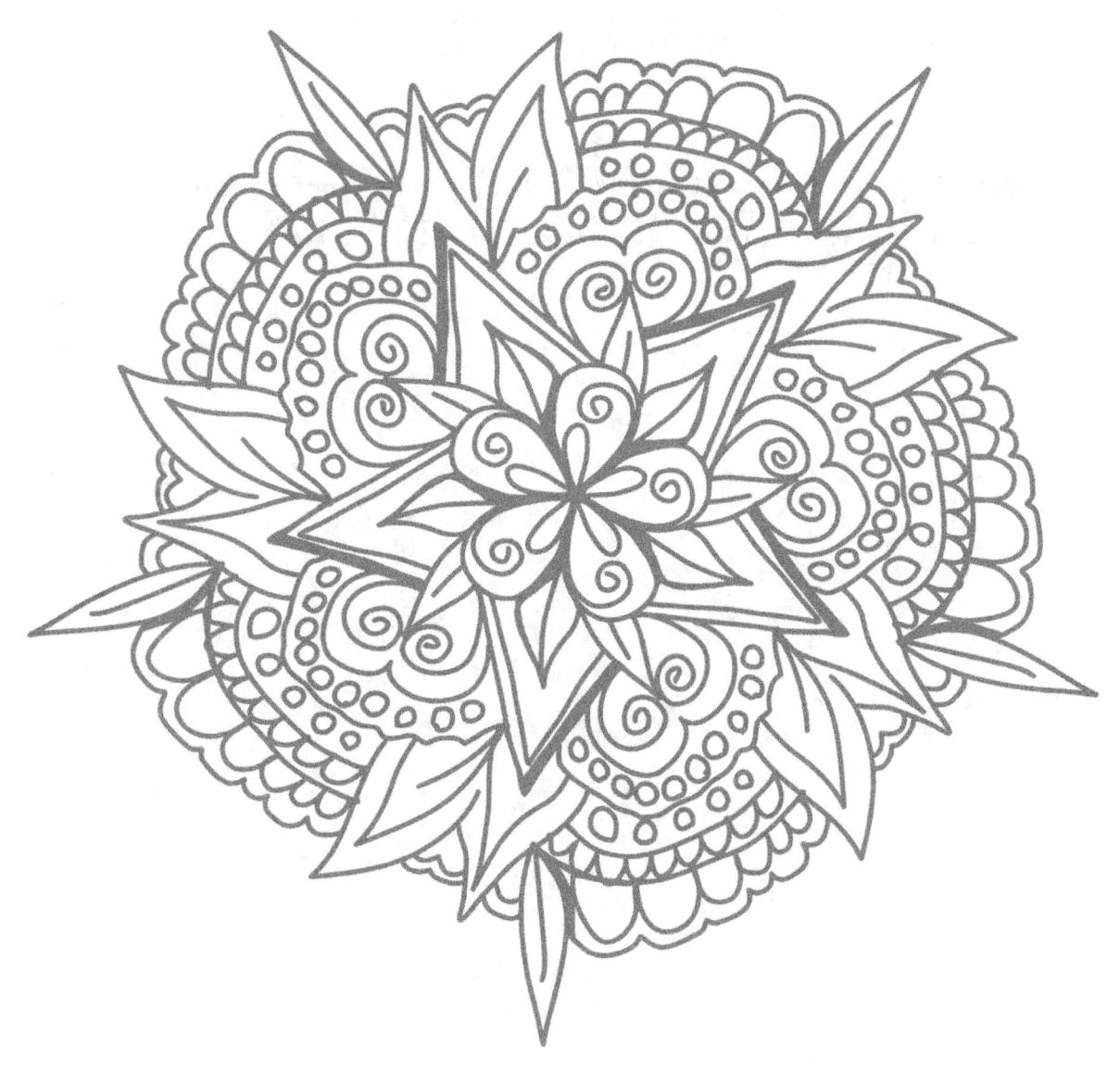

Date _____

> If you want something new, you have to stop doing something old.
> -Peter F. Drucker

MORNING HABITS

What are the habits I want to build, increase or pay attention to? Sleep, water, meditation and journaling are the ones that are high on my list, what else do you want to add?

- [ ] 1. My time to get up is _____ am.
- [ ] 2. I will drink _____ glasses of water.
- [ ] 3. I did _____ minutes of Meditation.
- [ ] 4. I Journaled this morning.
- [ ] 5. _____
- [ ] 6. _____

Today's Creative Pursuit

What creativity will I pursue today? Baking, decorating, coloring, painting, music, creating software or a spreadsheet? The possibilities are endless.

_____
_____
_____

Today's Affirmations

Today's affirmations? I am creative, I am pursuing my dreams today, I am open to possibilities. What positive, present, personal statement are you making for yourself today? Repeat it at least 3 times today.

_____
_____
_____

One action I will take today to make myself or my life better.
Today I will try a new food, today I will go to the gym, today I will send that application, the possibilities are endless. What will you do today to make you life better?

_____
_____

One thing I will do today that is slightly out of my comfort zone.
Those scary things that you think you can't do. What is the worst that will happen? Make that phone call, ask for that raise, create that video, do what ever it takes to pull yourself out of your comfort zone, just one small thing each day will make a huge difference.

_____

Doodle of the Day

MUSIC

Creativity is a drug I cannot live without. -Cecil B. DeMille

How does this quote make you feel?

Notes

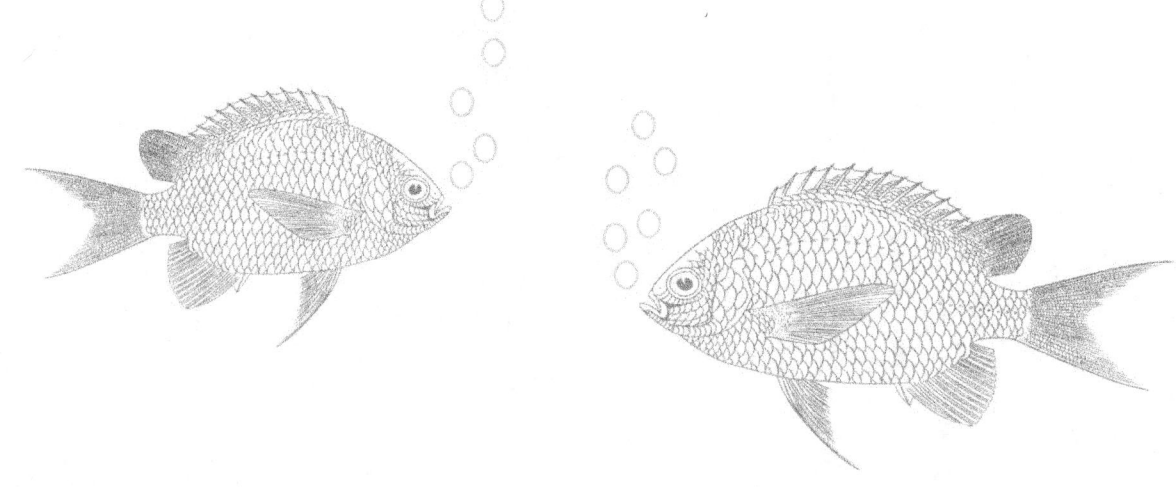

Date _____

> An invasion of armies can be resisted, but not an idea whose time has come.
> -Victor Hugo

MORNING HABITS

What are the habits I want to build, increase or pay attention to? Sleep, water, meditation and journaling are the ones that are high on my list, what else do you want to add?

- [ ] 1. My time to get up is _____ am.
- [ ] 2. I will drink _____ glasses of water.
- [ ] 3. I did _____ minutes of Meditation.
- [ ] 4. I Journaled this morning.
- [ ] 5. _____
- [ ] 6. _____

Today's Creative Pursuit

What creativity will I pursue today? Baking, decorating, coloring, painting, music, creating software or a spreadsheet? The possibilities are endless.

_____
_____
_____

Today's Affirmations

Today's affirmations? I am creative, I am pursuing my dreams today, I am open to possibilities. What positive, present, personal statement are you making for yourself today? Repeat it at least 3 times today.

_____
_____
_____

One action I will take today to make myself or my life better.

Today I will try a new food, today I will go to the gym, today I will send that application, the possibilities are endless. What will you do today to make you life better?

_____
_____

One thing I will do today that is slightly out of my comfort zone.

Those scary things that you think you can't do. What is the worst that will happen? Make that phone call, ask for that raise, create that video, do what ever it takes to pull yourself out of your comfort zone, just one small thing each day will make a huge difference.

_____
_____

Doodle of the Day

The creative person is willing to live with ambiguity. -Abe Tannenbaum

How does this quote make you feel?

Notes

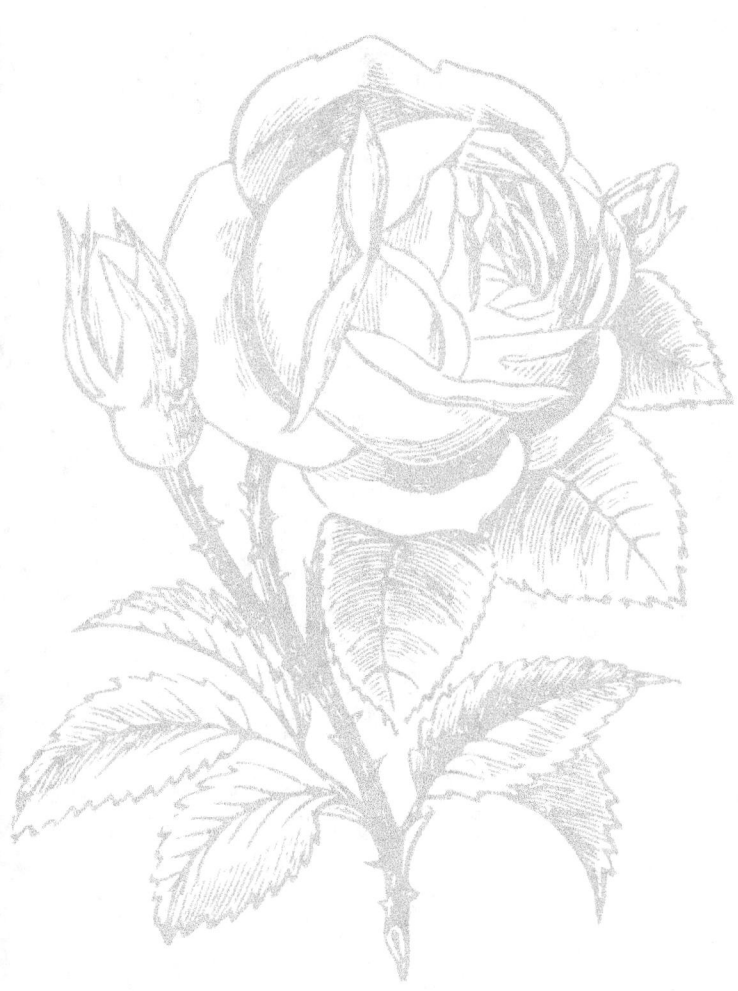

Date _____

> There is no doubt that creativity is the most important human resource of all.
> -Edward de Bono

MORNING HABITS

What are the habits I want to build, increase or pay attention to? Sleep, water, meditation and journaling are the ones that are high on my list, what else do you want to add?

- [ ] 1. My time to get up is _____ am.
- [ ] 2. I will drink _____ glasses of water.
- [ ] 3. I did _____ minutes of Meditation.
- [ ] 4. I Journaled this morning.
- [ ] 5. _____
- [ ] 6. _____

Today's Creative Pursuit

What creativity will I pursue today? Baking, decorating, coloring, painting, music, creating software or a spreadsheet? The possibilities are endless.

_____
_____
_____

Today's Affirmations

Today's affirmations? I am creative, I am pursuing my dreams today, I am open to possibilities. What positive, present, personal statement are you making for yourself today? Repeat it at least 3 times today.

_____
_____
_____

One action I will take today to make myself or my life better.

Today I will try a new food, today I will go to the gym, today I will send that application, the possibilities are endless. What will you do today to make you life better?

_____
_____

One thing I will do today that is slightly out of my comfort zone.

Those scary things that you think you can't do. What is the worst that will happen? Make that phone call, ask for that raise, create that video, do what ever it takes to pull yourself out of your comfort zone, just one small thing each day will make a huge difference.

_____
_____

Doodle of the Day

There is no innovation and creativity without failure. Period. -Brene Brown

How does this quote make you feel?

Notes

Date _____

> Every child is an artist, the problem is
> staying an artist when you grow up.
> -Pablo Picasso

MORNING HABITS

What are the habits I want to build, increase or pay attention to? Sleep, water, meditation and journaling are the ones that are high on my list, what else do you want to add?

☐ 1. My time to get up is _____ am.
☐ 2. I will drink _____ glasses of water.
☐ 3. I did _____ minutes of Meditation.
☐ 4. I Journaled this morning.
☐ 5. _____
☐ 6. _____

Today's Creative Pursuit

What creativity will I pursue today? Baking, decorating, coloring, painting, music, creating software or a spreadsheet? The possibilities are endless.

_____
_____
_____

Today's Affirmations

Today's affirmations? I am creative, I am pursuing my dreams today, I am open to possibilities. What positive, present, personal statement are you making for yourself today? Repeat it at least 3 times today.

_____
_____
_____

One action I will take today to make myself or my life better.

Today I will try a new food, today I will go to the gym, today I will send that application, the possibilities are endless. What will you do today to make you life better?

_____
_____

One thing I will do today that is slightly out of my comfort zone.

Those scary things that you think you can't do. What is the worst that will happen? Make that phone call, ask for that raise, create that video, do what ever it takes to pull yourself out of your comfort zone, just one small thing each day will make a huge difference.

_____
_____

Doodle of the Day

Oh, the thinks you can think up if only you try. -Dr. Seuss

How does this quote make you feel?

Notes

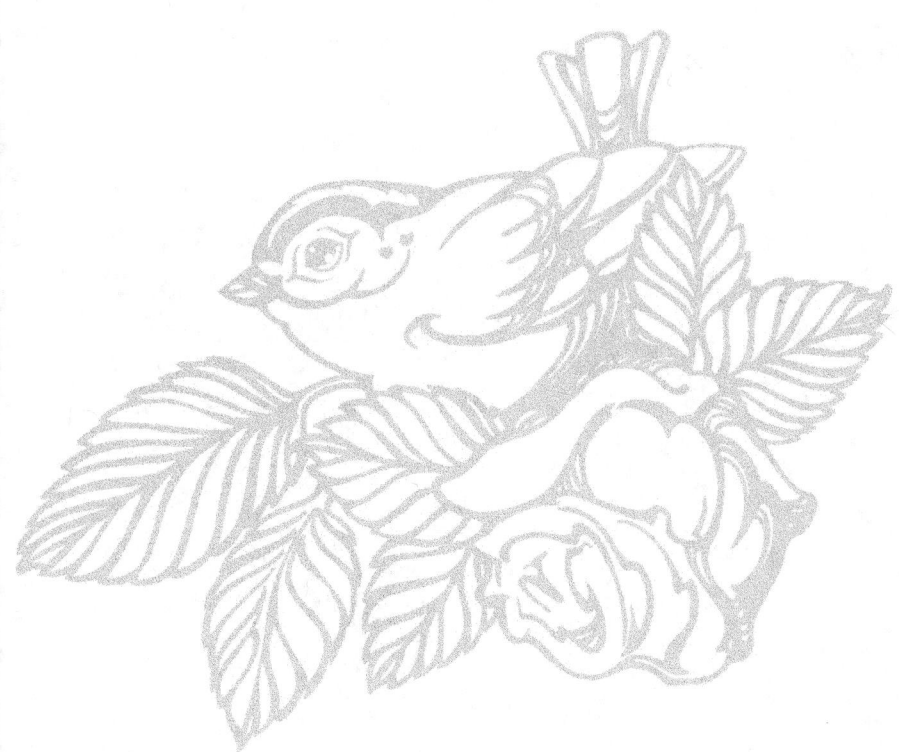

Date _____

Creativity can solve almost any problem.
-George Lois

MORNING HABITS

What are the habits I want to build, increase or pay attention to? Sleep, water , meditation and journaling are the ones that are high on my list, what else do you want to add?

☐ 1. My time to get up is _____ am.
☐ 2. I will drink _____ glasses of water.
☐ 3. I did _____ minutes of Meditation.
☐ 4. I Journaled this morning.
☐ 5. _____
☐ 6. _____

Today's Creative Pursuit

What creativity will I pursue today? Baking, decorating, coloring, painting, music, creating software or a spreadsheet? The possibilities are endless.

_____
_____
_____

Today's Affirmations

Today's affirmations? I am creative, I am pursuing my dreams today, I am open to possibilities. What positive, present, personal statement are you making for yourself today? Repeat it at least 3 times today.

_____
_____
_____

One action I will take today to make myself or my life better.

Today I will try a new food, today I will go to the gym, today I will send that application, the possibilities are endless. What will you do today to make you life better?

_____
_____

One thing I will do today that is slightly out of my comfort zone.

Those scary things that you think you can't do. What is the worst that will happen? Make that phone call, ask for that raise, create that video, do what ever it takes to pull yourself out of your comfort zone, just one small thing each day will make a huge difference.

_____

Doodle of the Day

Every day is an opportunity to be creative. -Innerspace

How does this quote make you feel?

Notes

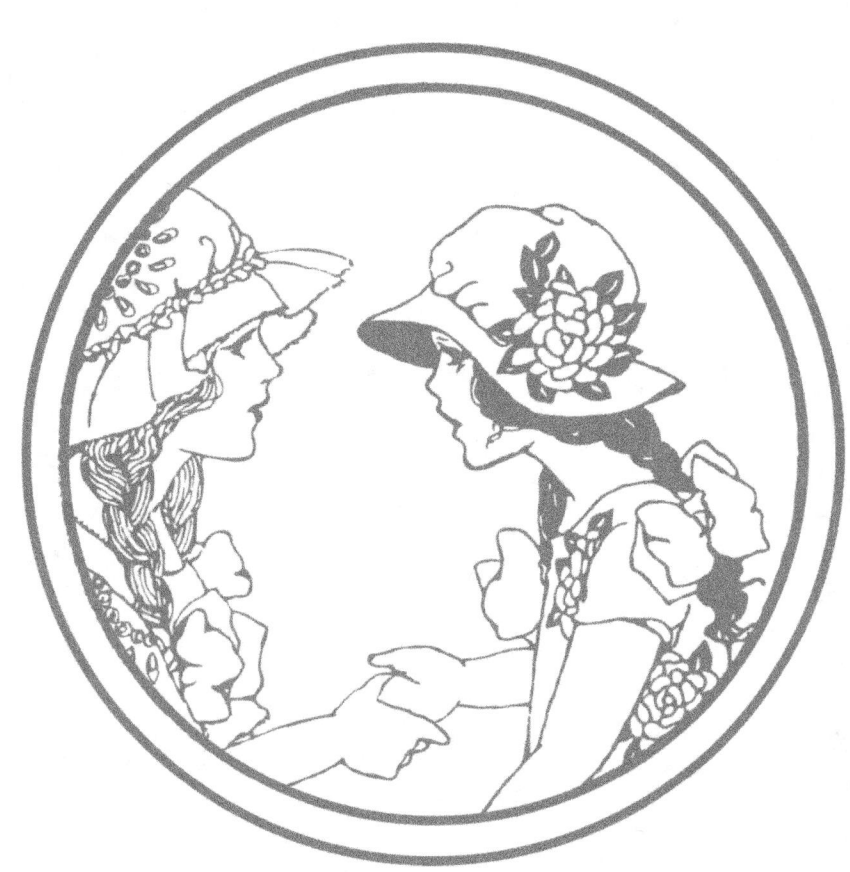

Date _____

Creative living is where Big Magic will always abide. -Elizabeth Gilbert

Today's Creative Pursuit

What creativity will I pursue today? Baking, decorating, coloring, painting, music, creating software or a spreadsheet? The possibilities are endless.

_____

_____

_____

MORNING HABITS

What are the habits I want to build, increase or pay attention to? Sleep, water, meditation and journaling are the ones that are high on my list, what else do you want to add?

- [ ] 1. My time to get up is _____ am.
- [ ] 2. I will drink _____ glasses of water.
- [ ] 3. I did _____ minutes of Meditation.
- [ ] 4. I Journaled this morning.
- [ ] 5. _____
- [ ] 6. _____

Today's Affirmations

Today's affirmations? I am creative, I am pursuing my dreams today, I am open to possibilities. What positive, present, personal statement are you making for yourself today? Repeat it at least 3 times today.

_____

_____

_____

One action I will take today to make myself or my life better.

Today I will try a new food, today I will go to the gym, today I will send that application, the possibilities are endless. What will you do today to make you life better?

_____

_____

One thing I will do today that is slightly out of my comfort zone.

Those scary things that you think you can't do. What is the worst that will happen? Make that phone call, ask for that raise, create that video, do what ever it takes to pull yourself out of your comfort zone, just one small thing each day will make a huge difference.

_____

_____

Doodle of the Day

Without freedom, there is no creation. -Jiddu Krishnamurti

How does this quote make you feel?

Notes

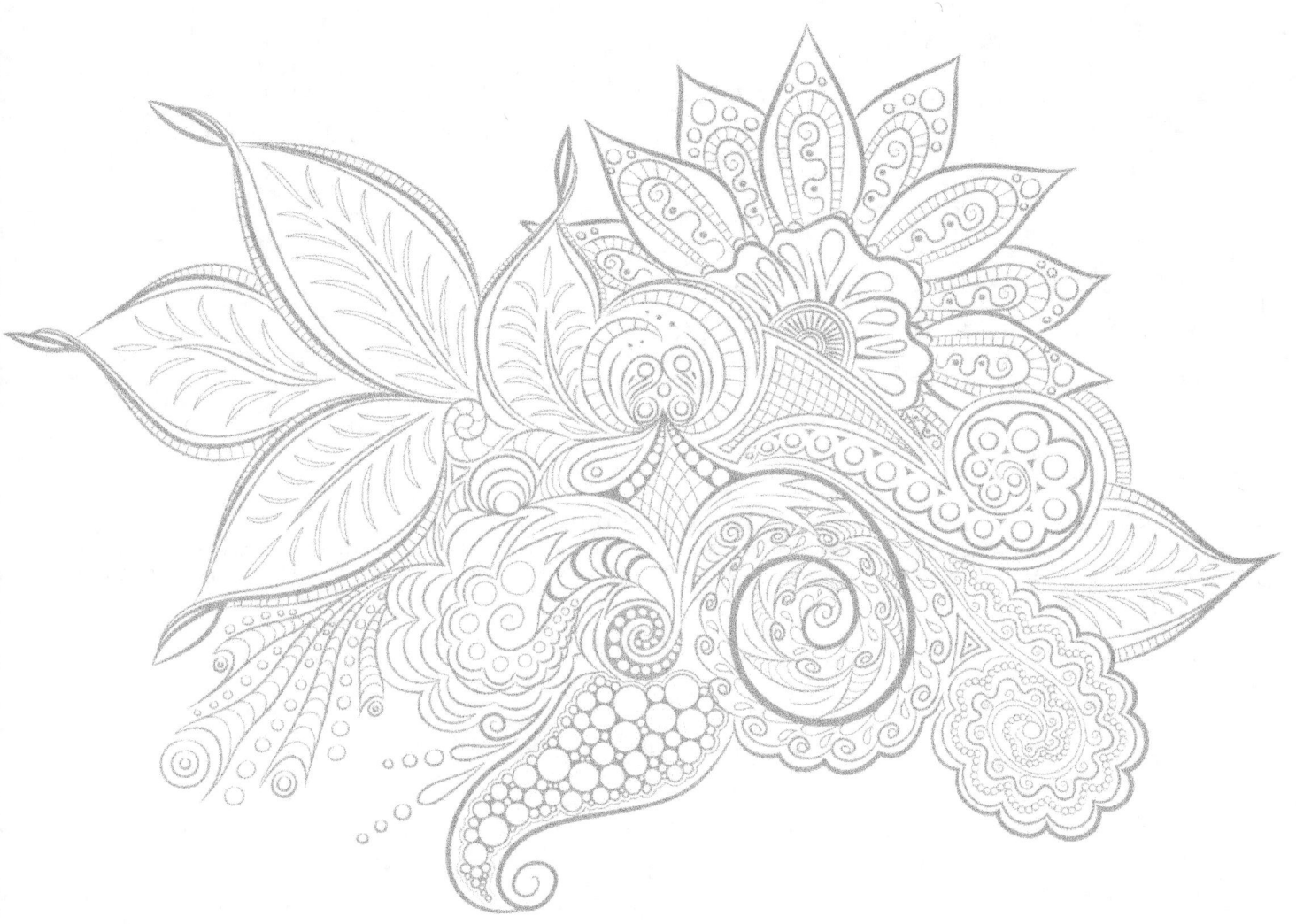

Date _____

> Creativity is allowing yourself to make mistakes. Art is knowing which ones to keep. -Scott Adams

Today's Creative Pursuit

What creativity will I pursue today? Baking, decorating, coloring, painting, music, creating software or a spreadsheet? The possibilities are endless.

_____
_____
_____

MORNING HABITS

What are the habits I want to build, increase or pay attention to? Sleep, water, meditation and journaling are the ones that are high on my list, what else do you want to add?

1. My time to get up is _____ am.
2. I will drink _____ glasses of water.
3. I did _____ minutes of Meditation.
4. I Journaled this morning.
5. _____
6. _____

Today's Affirmations

Today's affirmations? I am creative, I am pursuing my dreams today, I am open to possibilities. What positive, present, personal statement are you making for yourself today? Repeat it at least 3 times today.

_____
_____
_____

One action I will take today to make myself or my life better.
Today I will try a new food, today I will go to the gym, today I will send that application, the possibilities are endless. What will you do today to make you life better?

_____
_____

One thing I will do today that is slightly out of my comfort zone.
Those scary things that you think you can't do. What is the worst that will happen? Make that phone call, ask for that raise, create that video, do what ever it takes to pull yourself out of your comfort zone, just one small thing each day will make a huge difference.

_____
_____

Doodle of the Day

Creativity is the natural order of life. -Julia Cameron

How does this quote make you feel?

Notes

Date _____

> Creativity is thinking up new things.
> Innovation is doing new things.
> -Theodore Levitt

Today's Creative Pursuit

What creativity will I pursue today? Baking, decorating, coloring, painting, music, creating software or a spreadsheet? The possibilities are endless.

_____
_____
_____

MORNING HABITS

What are the habits I want to build, increase or pay attention to? Sleep, water, meditation and journaling are the ones that are high on my list, what else do you want to add?

☐ 1. My time to get up is _____ am.
☐ 2. I will drink _____ glasses of water.
☐ 3. I did _____ minutes of Meditation.
☐ 4. I Journaled this morning.
☐ 5. _____
☐ 6. _____

Today's Affirmations

Today's affirmations? I am creative, I am pursuing my dreams today, I am open to possibilities. What positive, present, personal statement are you making for yourself today? Repeat it at least 3 times today.

_____
_____
_____

One action I will take today to make myself or my life better.

Today I will try a new food, today I will go to the gym, today I will send that application, the possibilities are endless. What will you do today to make you life better?

_____
_____

One thing I will do today that is slightly out of my comfort zone.

Those scary things that you think you can't do. What is the worst that will happen? Make that phone call, ask for that raise, create that video, do what ever it takes to pull yourself out of your comfort zone, just one small thing each day will make a huge difference.

_____
_____

Doodle of the Day

I don't know what I think until I write about it. -Joan Didion

How does this quote make you feel?

Notes

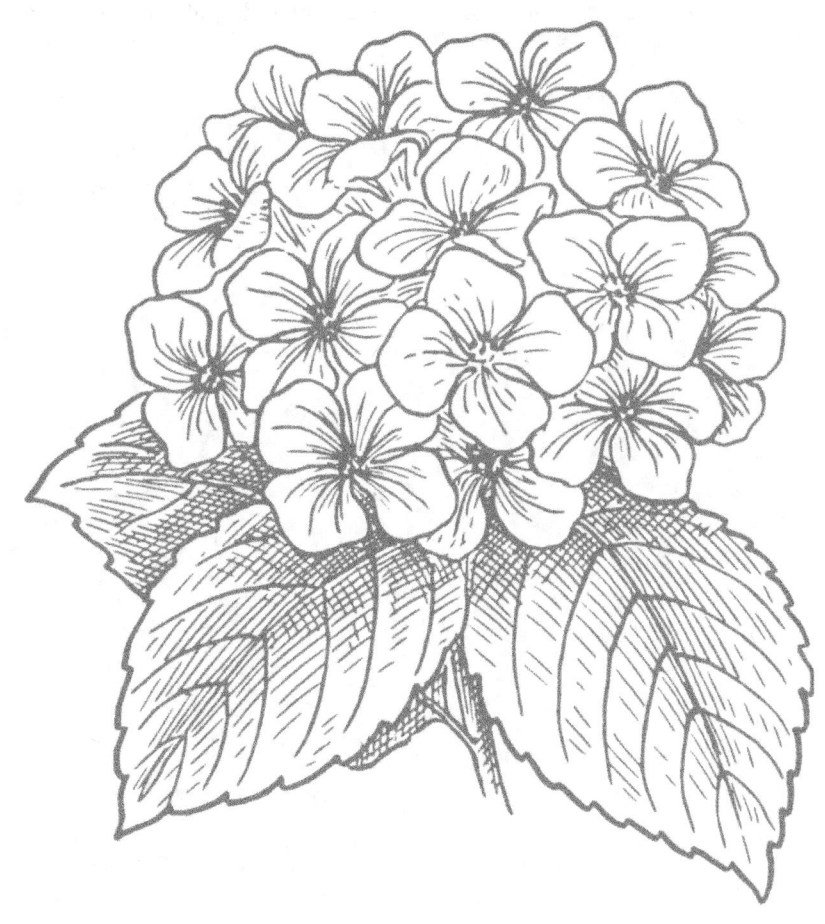

Date _____

> Creativity can be described as letting go of certainties. -Gail Sheehy

Today's Creative Pursuit

What creativity will I pursue today? Baking, decorating, coloring, painting, music, creating software or a spreadsheet? The possibilities are endless.

_____
_____
_____

MORNING HABITS

What are the habits I want to build, increase or pay attention to? Sleep, water, meditation and journaling are the ones that are high on my list, what else do you want to add?

1. My time to get up is _____ am.
2. I will drink _____ glasses of water.
3. I did _____ minutes of Meditation.
4. I Journaled this morning.
5. _____
6. _____

Today's Affirmations

Today's affirmations? I am creative, I am pursuing my dreams today, I am open to possibilities. What positive, present, personal statement are you making for yourself today? Repeat it at least 3 times today.

_____
_____
_____

One action I will take today to make myself or my life better.
Today I will try a new food, today I will go to the gym, today I will send that application, the possibilities are endless. What will you do today to make you life better?

_____
_____

One thing I will do today that is slightly out of my comfort zone.
Those scary things that you think you can't do. What is the worst that will happen? Make that phone call, ask for that raise, create that video, do what ever it takes to pull yourself out of your comfort zone, just one small thing each day will make a huge difference.

_____
_____

Doodle of the Day

A creative life is an amplified life. -Elizabeth Gilbert

How does this quote make you feel?

Notes

Date _____

> I've found constancy and balance between creativity and normality.
> -Julian Lennon

MORNING HABITS

What are the habits I want to build, increase or pay attention to? Sleep, water, meditation and journaling are the ones that are high on my list, what else do you want to add?

- [ ] 1. My time to get up is _____ am.
- [ ] 2. I will drink _____ glasses of water.
- [ ] 3. I did _____ minutes of Meditation.
- [ ] 4. I Journaled this morning.
- [ ] 5. _____
- [ ] 6. _____

Today's Creative Pursuit

What creativity will I pursue today? Baking, decorating, coloring, painting, music, creating software or a spreadsheet? The possibilities are endless.

_____
_____
_____

Today's Affirmations

Today's affirmations? I am creative, I am pursuing my dreams today, I am open to possibilities. What positive, present, personal statement are you making for yourself today? Repeat it at least 3 times today.

_____
_____
_____

One action I will take today to make myself or my life better.

Today I will try a new food, today I will go to the gym, today I will send that application, the possibilities are endless. What will you do today to make you life better?

_____
_____

One thing I will do today that is slightly out of my comfort zone.

Those scary things that you think you can't do. What is the worst that will happen? Make that phone call, ask for that raise, create that video, do what ever it takes to pull yourself out of your comfort zone, just one small thing each day will make a huge difference.

_____
_____

Doodle of the Day

It is better to fail in originality, than to succeed in imitation. -Herman Melville

How does this quote make you feel?

Notes

Date _____

> Creativity comes from trust. Trust your instincts. And never hope more than you work. -Rita Mae Brown

MORNING HABITS

What are the habits I want to build, increase or pay attention to? Sleep, water, meditation and journaling are the ones that are high on my list, what else do you want to add?

- [ ] 1. My time to get up is _____ am.
- [ ] 2. I will drink _____ glasses of water.
- [ ] 3. I did _____ minutes of Meditation.
- [ ] 4. I Journaled this morning.
- [ ] 5. _____
- [ ] 6. _____

Today's Creative Pursuit

What creativity will I pursue today? Baking, decorating, coloring, painting, music, creating software or a spreadsheet? The possibilities are endless.

_____
_____
_____

Today's Affirmations

Today's affirmations? I am creative, I am pursuing my dreams today, I am open to possibilities. What positive, present, personal statement are you making for yourself today? Repeat it at least 3 times today.

_____
_____
_____

One action I will take today to make myself or my life better.

Today I will try a new food, today I will go to the gym, today I will send that application, the possibilities are endless. What will you do today to make you life better?

_____
_____

One thing I will do today that is slightly out of my comfort zone.

Those scary things that you think you can't do. What is the worst that will happen? Make that phone call, ask for that raise, create that video, do what ever it takes to pull yourself out of your comfort zone, just one small thing each day will make a huge difference.

_____
_____

Doodle of the Day

Creativity is piercing the mundane to find the marvelous. -Bill Moyers

How does this quote make you feel?

Notes

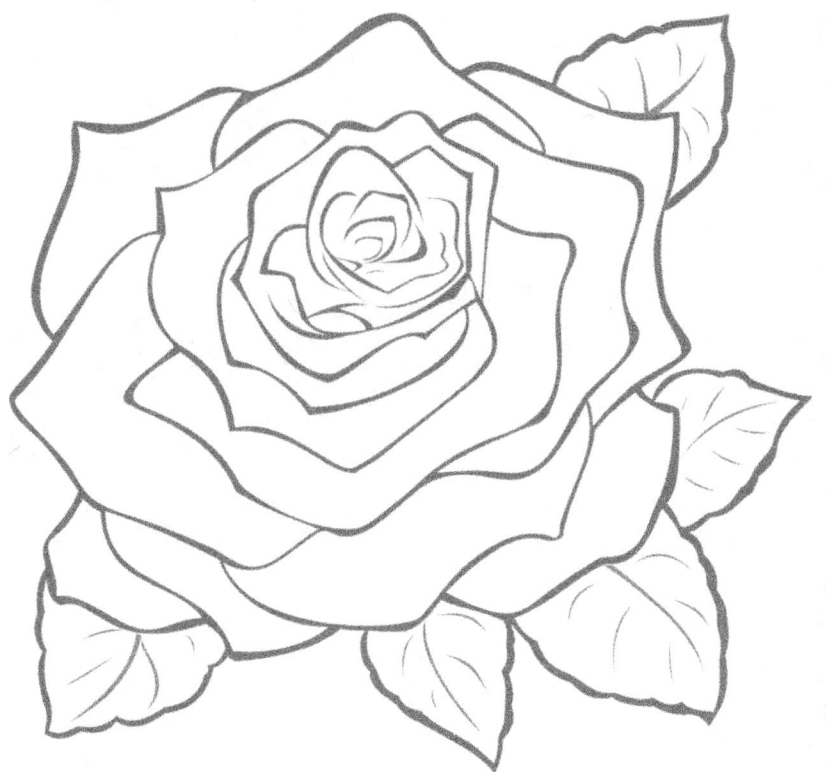

Date _____

> Politics is the art of the possible; creativity is the art of the impossible.
> -Ben Okri

MORNING HABITS

What are the habits I want to build, increase or pay attention to? Sleep, water, meditation and journaling are the ones that are high on my list, what else do you want to add?

☐ 1. My time to get up is _____ am.
☐ 2. I will drink _____ glasses of water.
☐ 3. I did _____ minutes of Meditation.
☐ 4. I Journaled this morning.
☐ 5. _____
☐ 6. _____

Today's Creative Pursuit

What creativity will I pursue today? Baking, decorating, coloring, painting, music, creating software or a spreadsheet? The possibilities are endless.

_____
_____
_____

Today's Affirmations

Today's affirmations? I am creative, I am pursuing my dreams today, I am open to possibilities. What positive, present, personal statement are you making for yourself today? Repeat it at least 3 times today.

_____
_____
_____

One action I will take today to make myself or my life better.

Today I will try a new food, today I will go to the gym, today I will send that application, the possibilities are endless. What will you do today to make you life better?

_____
_____

One thing I will do today that is slightly out of my comfort zone.

Those scary things that you think you can't do. What is the worst that will happen? Make that phone call, ask for that raise, create that video, do what ever it takes to pull yourself out of your comfort zone, just one small thing each day will make a huge difference.

_____
_____

Doodle of the Day

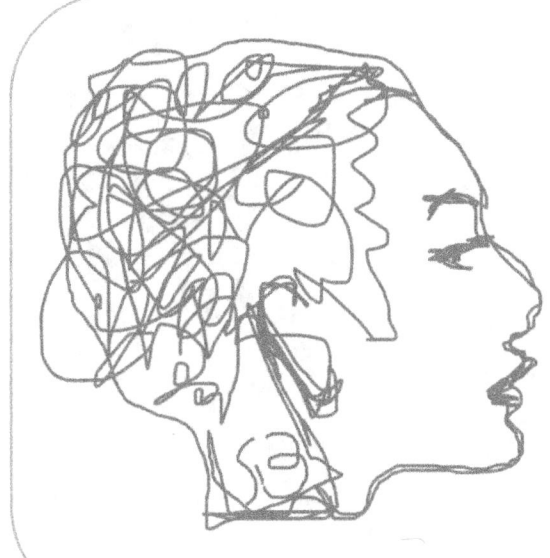

We have the capacity for infinite creativity. -Jackie Gleason

How does this quote make you feel?

Notes

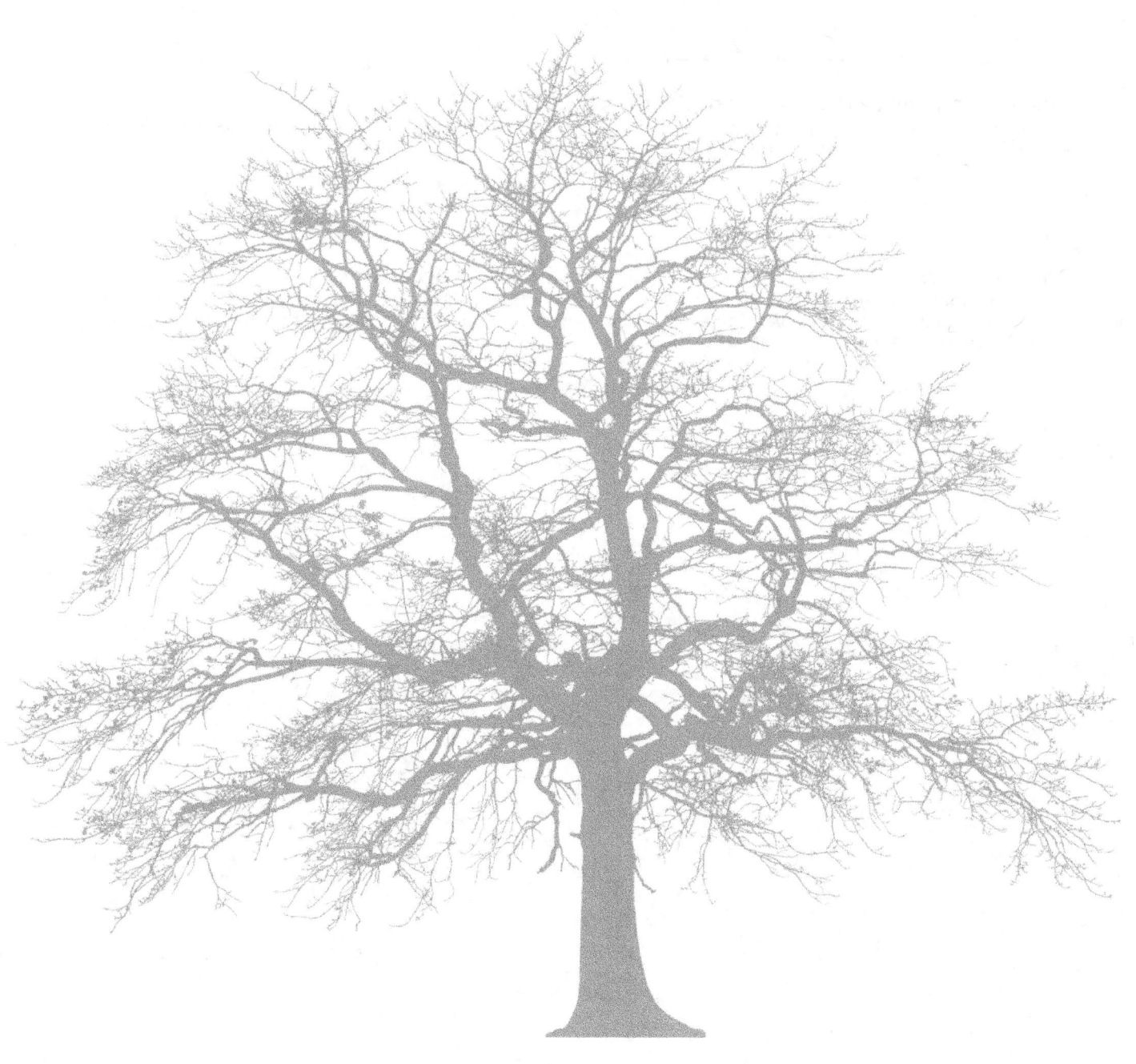

Date _____

> You can't use up creativity. The more you use, the more you have.
> -Maya Angelou

MORNING HABITS

What are the habits I want to build, increase or pay attention to? Sleep, water, meditation and journaling are the ones that are high on my list, what else do you want to add?

- [ ] 1. My time to get up is _____ am.
- [ ] 2. I will drink _____ glasses of water.
- [ ] 3. I did _____ minutes of Meditation.
- [ ] 4. I Journaled this morning.
- [ ] 5. _____
- [ ] 6. _____

Today's Creative Pursuit

What creativity will I pursue today? Baking, decorating, coloring, painting, music, creating software or a spreadsheet? The possibilities are endless.

_____
_____

Today's Affirmations

Today's affirmations? I am creative, I am pursuing my dreams today, I am open to possibilities. What positive, present, personal statement are you making for yourself today? Repeat it at least 3 times today.

_____
_____
_____

One action I will take today to make myself or my life better.

Today I will try a new food, today I will go to the gym, today I will send that application, the possibilities are endless. What will you do today to make you life better?

_____
_____

One thing I will do today that is slightly out of my comfort zone.

Those scary things that you think you can't do. What is the worst that will happen? Make that phone call, ask for that raise, create that video, do what ever it takes to pull yourself out of your comfort zone, just one small thing each day will make a huge difference.

_____

Doodle of the Day

Controversy is part of the nature of art and creativity. -Yoko Ono

How does this quote make you feel?

Notes

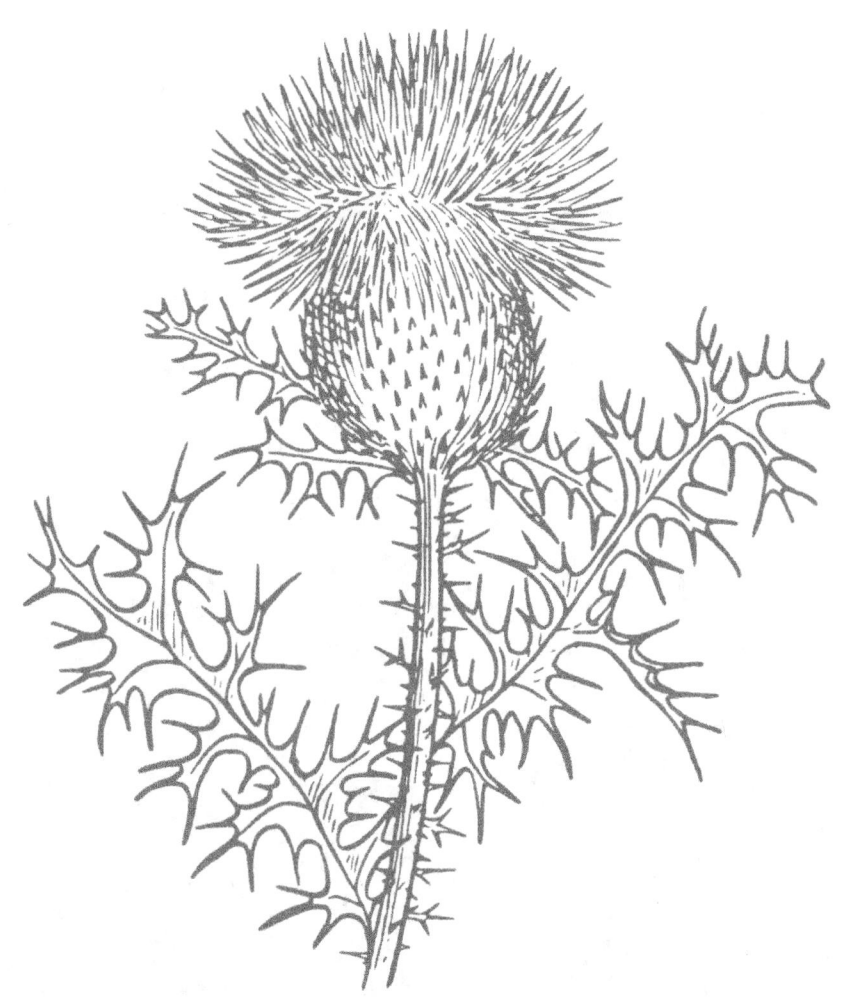

Date _____

> Creativity itself doesn't care at all about results – the only thing it craves is the process. -Elizabeth Gilbert

MORNING HABITS

What are the habits I want to build, increase or pay attention to? Sleep, water, meditation and journaling are the ones that are high on my list, what else do you want to add?

☐ 1. My time to get up is _____ am.
☐ 2. I will drink _____ glasses of water.
☐ 3. I did _____ minutes of Meditation.
☐ 4. I Journaled this morning.
☐ 5. _____
☐ 6. _____

Today's Creative Pursuit

What creativity will I pursue today? Baking, decorating, coloring, painting, music, creating software or a spreadsheet? The possibilities are endless.

_____
_____
_____

Today's Affirmations

Today's affirmations? I am creative, I am pursuing my dreams today, I am open to possibilities. What positive, present, personal statement are you making for yourself today? Repeat it at least 3 times today.

_____
_____
_____

One action I will take today to make myself or my life better.

Today I will try a new food, today I will go to the gym, today I will send that application, the possibilities are endless. What will you do today to make you life better?

_____
_____

One thing I will do today that is slightly out of my comfort zone.

Those scary things that you think you can't do. What is the worst that will happen? Make that phone call, ask for that raise, create that video, do what ever it takes to pull yourself out of your comfort zone, just one small thing each day will make a huge difference.

_____
_____

Doodle of the Day

Can't kills creativity! -Camille Paglia

How does this quote make you feel?

Notes

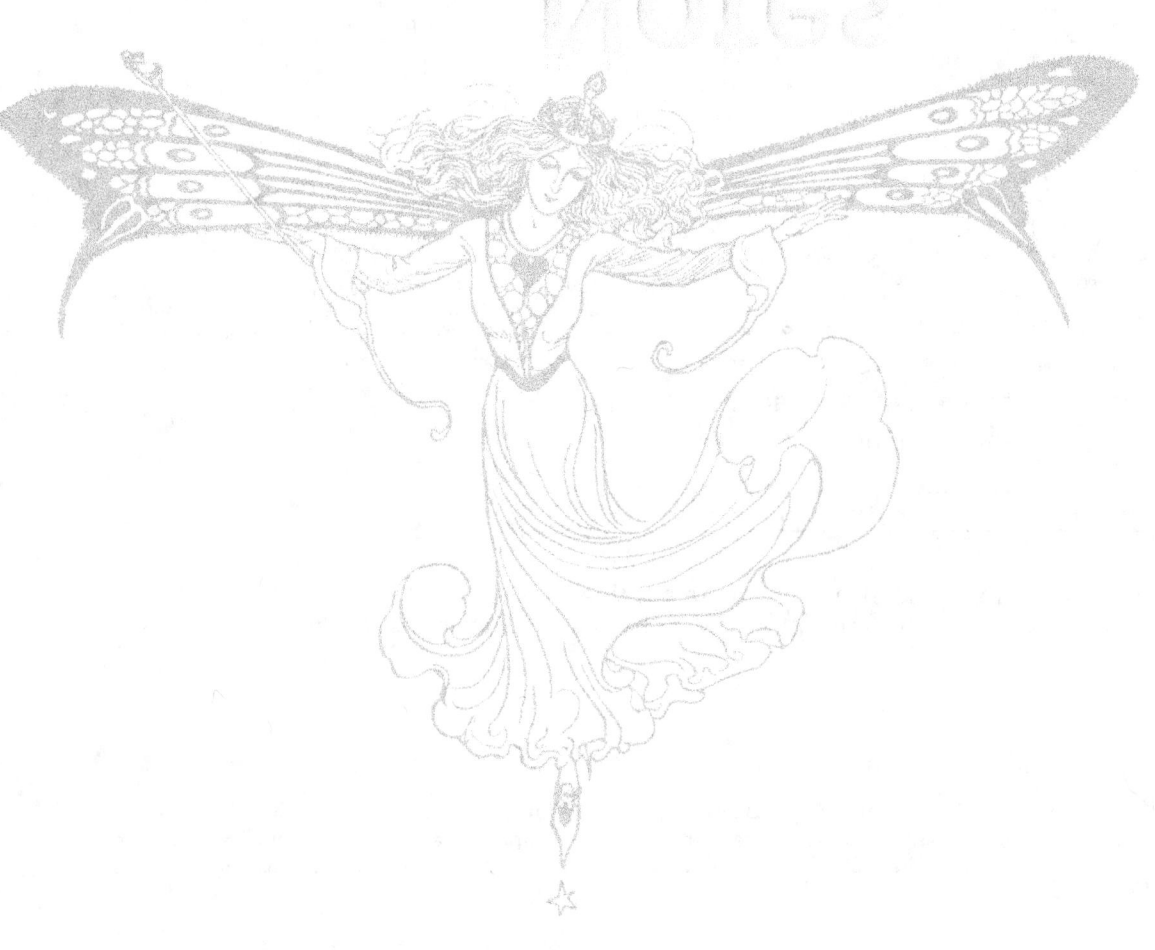

Date _____

> The refusal to be creative is self-will and is counter to our true nature.
> -Julia Cameron

MORNING HABITS

What are the habits I want to build, increase or pay attention to? Sleep, water, meditation and journaling are the ones that are high on my list, what else do you want to add?

- [ ] 1. My time to get up is _____ am.
- [ ] 2. I will drink _____ glasses of water.
- [ ] 3. I did _____ minutes of Meditation.
- [ ] 4. I Journaled this morning.
- [ ] 5. _____
- [ ] 6. _____

Today's Creative Pursuit

What creativity will I pursue today? Baking, decorating, coloring, painting, music, creating software or a spreadsheet? The possibilities are endless.

_____
_____
_____

Today's Affirmations

Today's affirmations? I am creative, I am pursuing my dreams today, I am open to possibilities. What positive, present, personal statement are you making for yourself today? Repeat it at least 3 times today.

_____
_____
_____

One action I will take today to make myself or my life better.

Today I will try a new food, today I will go to the gym, today I will send that application, the possibilities are endless. What will you do today to make you life better?

_____
_____

One thing I will do today that is slightly out of my comfort zone.

Those scary things that you think you can't do. What is the worst that will happen? Make that phone call, ask for that raise, create that video, do what ever it takes to pull yourself out of your comfort zone, just one small thing each day will make a huge difference.

_____
_____

Doodle of the Day

To be creative means to be in love with life. -Osho

How does this quote make you feel?

Notes

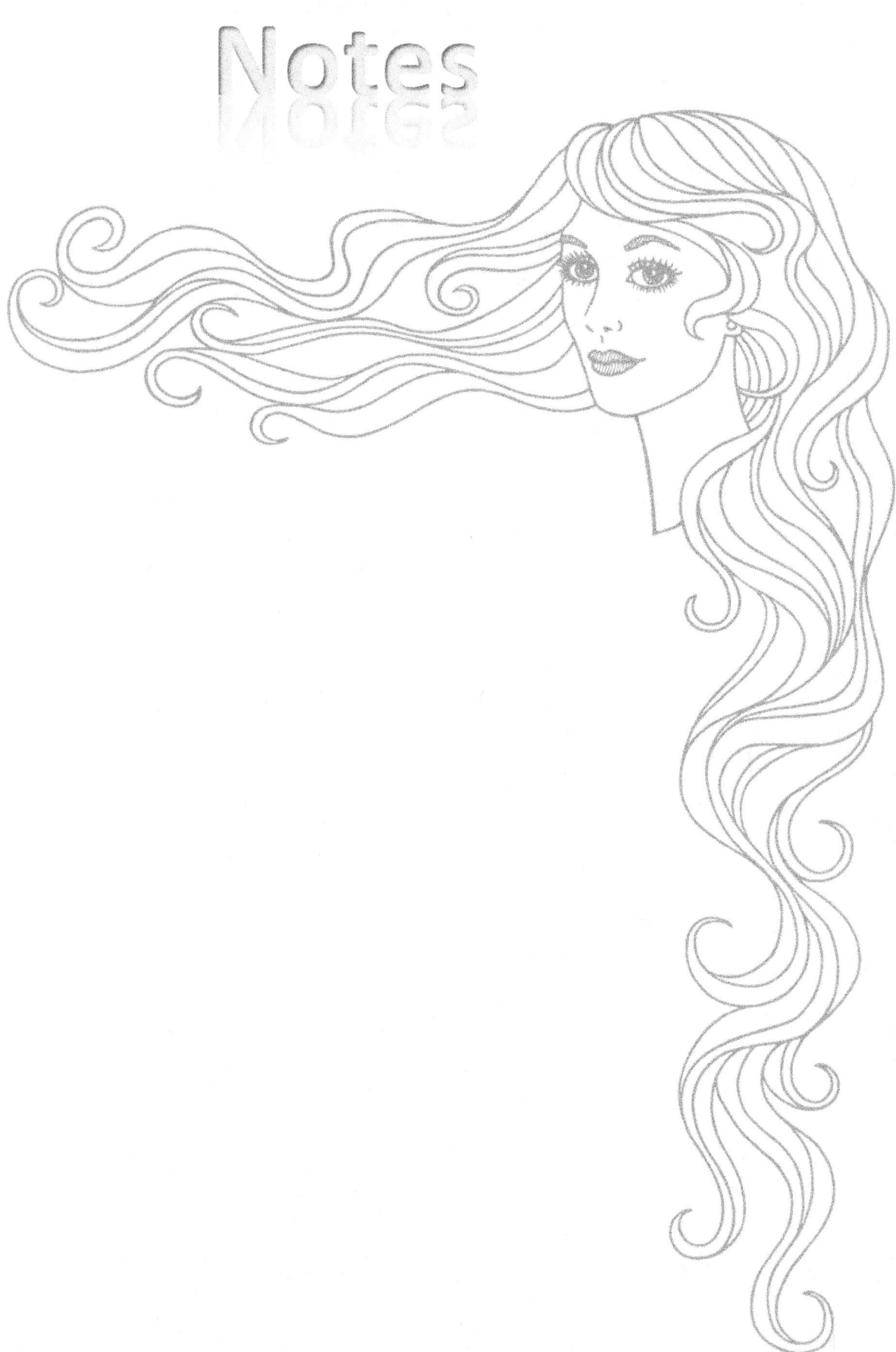

Date _____

> Originality is the essence of true scholarship. Creativity is the soul of the true scholar. -Nnamdi Azikiwe

MORNING HABITS

What are the habits I want to build, increase or pay attention to? Sleep, water, meditation and journaling are the ones that are high on my list, what else do you want to add?

- [ ] 1. My time to get up is _____ am.
- [ ] 2. I will drink _____ glasses of water.
- [ ] 3. I did _____ minutes of Meditation.
- [ ] 4. I Journaled this morning.
- [ ] 5. _____
- [ ] 6. _____

Today's Creative Pursuit

What creativity will I pursue today? Baking, decorating, coloring, painting, music, creating software or a spreadsheet? The possibilities are endless.

_____
_____
_____

Today's Affirmations

Today's affirmations? I am creative, I am pursuing my dreams today, I am open to possibilities. What positive, present, personal statement are you making for yourself today? Repeat it at least 3 times today.

_____
_____
_____

One action I will take today to make myself or my life better.

Today I will try a new food, today I will go to the gym, today I will send that application, the possibilities are endless. What will you do today to make you life better?

_____
_____

One thing I will do today that is slightly out of my comfort zone.

Those scary things that you think you can't do. What is the worst that will happen? Make that phone call, ask for that raise, create that video, do what ever it takes to pull yourself out of your comfort zone, just one small thing each day will make a huge difference.

_____
_____

Doodle of the Day

Punishing honest mistakes stifles creativity. -Ross Perot

How does this quote make you feel?

Notes

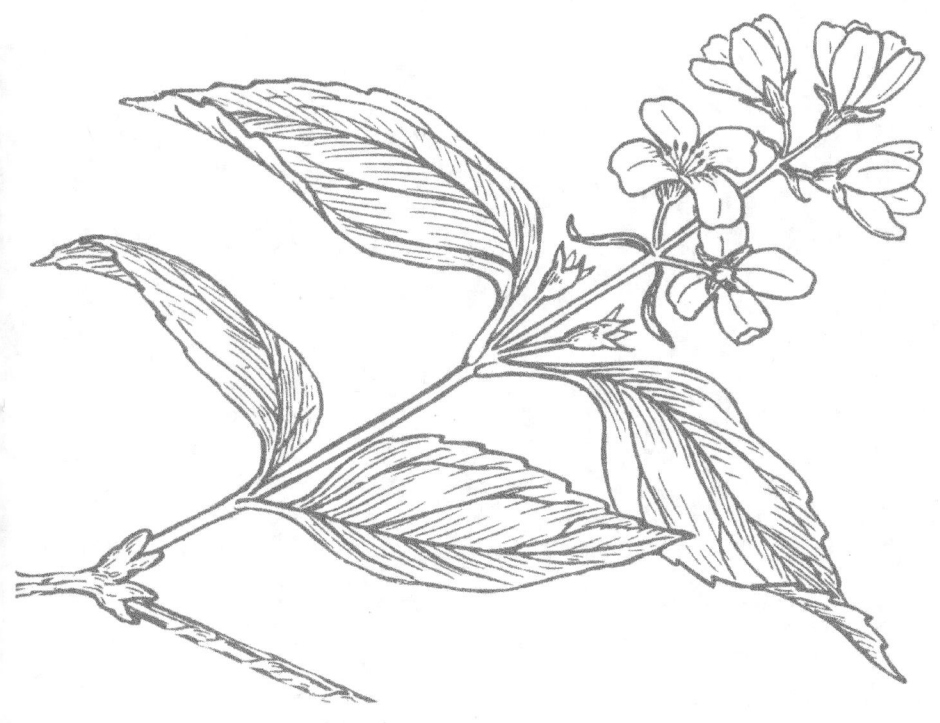

Date _____

> Creativity comes from looking for the unexpected and stepping outside your own experience. -Masaru Ibuka

Today's Creative Pursuit

What creativity will I pursue today? Baking, decorating, coloring, painting, music, creating software or a spreadsheet? The possibilities are endless.

_____
_____
_____

MORNING HABITS

What are the habits I want to build, increase or pay attention to? Sleep, water, meditation and journaling are the ones that are high on my list, what else do you want to add?

- [ ] 1. My time to get up is _____ am.
- [ ] 2. I will drink _____ glasses of water.
- [ ] 3. I did _____ minutes of Meditation.
- [ ] 4. I Journaled this morning.
- [ ] 5. _____
- [ ] 6. _____

Today's Affirmations

Today's affirmations? I am creative, I am pursuing my dreams today, I am open to possibilities. What positive, present, personal statement are you making for yourself today? Repeat it at least 3 times today.

_____
_____
_____

One action I will take today to make myself or my life better.
Today I will try a new food, today I will go to the gym, today I will send that application, the possibilities are endless. What will you do today to make you life better?

_____
_____

One thing I will do today that is slightly out of my comfort zone.
Those scary things that you think you can't do. What is the worst that will happen? Make that phone call, ask for that raise, create that video, do what ever it takes to pull yourself out of your comfort zone, just one small thing each day will make a huge difference.

_____
_____

Doodle of the Day

The artistry and the creativity in a story are better than any drugs.
-Wentworth Miller

How does this quote make you feel?

Notes

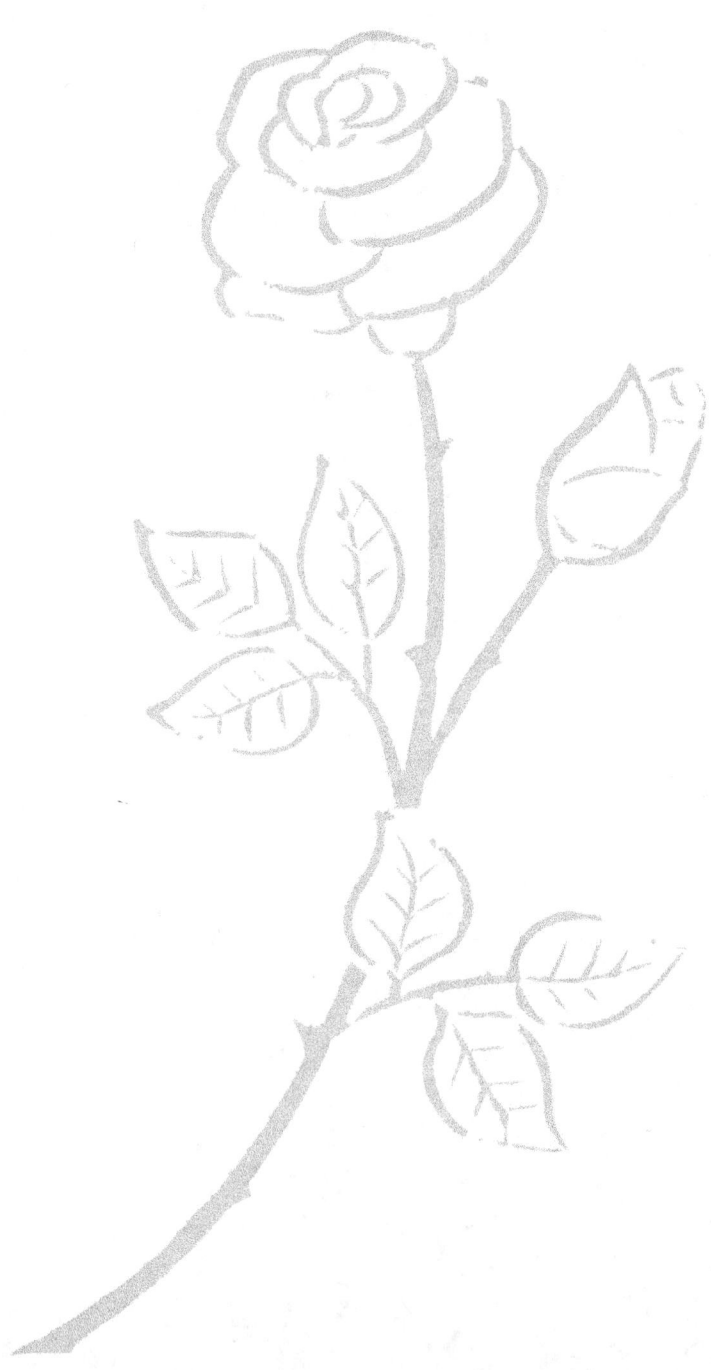

Date _____

> Clean out a corner of your mind and creativity will instantly fill it.
> -Dee Hock

Today's Creative Pursuit

What creativity will I pursue today? Baking, decorating, coloring, painting, music, creating software or a spreadsheet? The possibilities are endless.

_____

_____

MORNING HABITS

What are the habits I want to build, increase or pay attention to? Sleep, water, meditation and journaling are the ones that are high on my list, what else do you want to add?

- [ ] 1. My time to get up is _____ am.
- [ ] 2. I will drink _____ glasses of water.
- [ ] 3. I did _____ minutes of Meditation.
- [ ] 4. I Journaled this morning.
- [ ] 5. _____
- [ ] 6. _____

Today's Affirmations

Today's affirmations? I am creative, I am pursuing my dreams today, I am open to possibilities. What positive, present, personal statement are you making for yourself today? Repeat it at least 3 times today.

_____

_____

One action I will take today to make myself or my life better.

Today I will try a new food, today I will go to the gym, today I will send that application, the possibilities are endless. What will you do today to make you life better?

_____

_____

One thing I will do today that is slightly out of my comfort zone.

Those scary things that you think you can't do. What is the worst that will happen? Make that phone call, ask for that raise, create that video, do what ever it takes to pull yourself out of your comfort zone, just one small thing each day will make a huge difference.

_____

_____

Doodle of the Day

I go wherever my creativity takes me. -Lil Wayne

How does this quote make you feel?

Notes

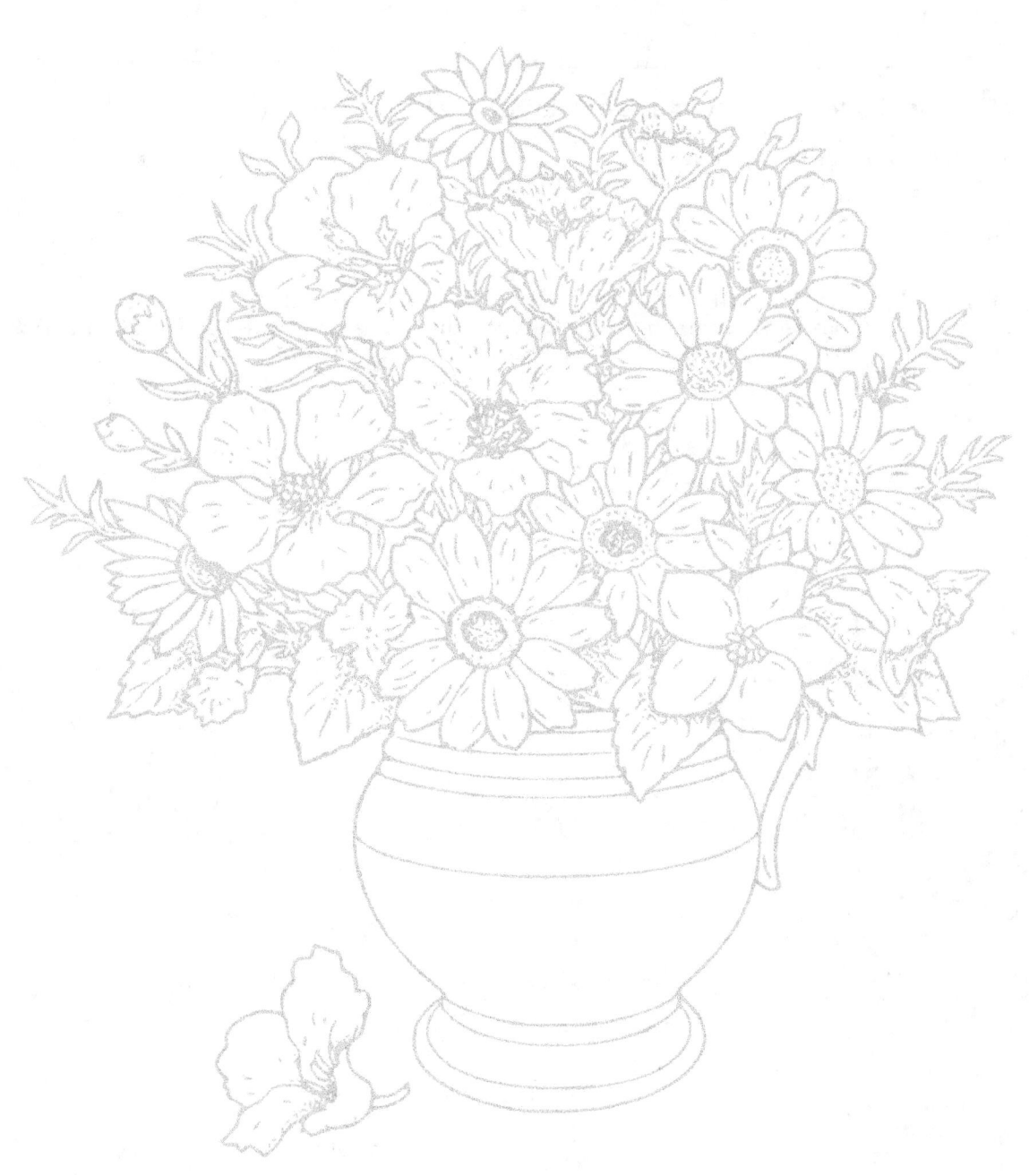

Date _____

> Creativity is what helps me escape a lot of my inner demons. -Demi Lovato

Today's Creative Pursuit

What creativity will I pursue today? Baking, decorating, coloring, painting, music, creating software or a spreadsheet? The possibilities are endless.

_____
_____
_____

MORNING HABITS

What are the habits I want to build, increase or pay attention to? Sleep, water, meditation and journaling are the ones that are high on my list, what else do you want to add?

1. My time to get up is _____ am.
2. I will drink _____ glasses of water.
3. I did _____ minutes of Meditation.
4. I Journaled this morning.
5. _____
6. _____

Today's Affirmations

Today's affirmations? I am creative, I am pursuing my dreams today, I am open to possibilities. What positive, present, personal statement are you making for yourself today? Repeat it at least 3 times today.

_____
_____
_____

One action I will take today to make myself or my life better.
Today I will try a new food, today I will go to the gym, today I will send that application, the possibilities are endless. What will you do today to make you life better?

_____

One thing I will do today that is slightly out of my comfort zone.
Those scary things that you think you can't do. What is the worst that will happen? Make that phone call, ask for that raise, create that video, do what ever it takes to pull yourself out of your comfort zone, just one small thing each day will make a huge difference.

_____

Doodle of the Day

Creativity is the sudden cessation of stupidity. -Edwin Land

How does this quote make you feel?

Notes

Date _____

> People have a God-given right to use their creativity to produce things that improve our lives. -Paul Ryan

MORNING HABITS

What are the habits I want to build, increase or pay attention to? Sleep, water, meditation and journaling are the ones that are high on my list, what else do you want to add?

- [ ] 1. My time to get up is _____ am.
- [ ] 2. I will drink _____ glasses of water.
- [ ] 3. I did _____ minutes of Meditation.
- [ ] 4. I Journaled this morning.
- [ ] 5. _____
- [ ] 6. _____

Today's Creative Pursuit

What creativity will I pursue today? Baking, decorating, coloring, painting, music, creating software or a spreadsheet? The possibilities are endless.

_____
_____
_____

Today's Affirmations

Today's affirmations? I am creative, I am pursuing my dreams today, I am open to possibilities. What positive, present, personal statement are you making for yourself today? Repeat it at least 3 times today.

_____
_____
_____

One action I will take today to make myself or my life better.

Today I will try a new food, today I will go to the gym, today I will send that application, the possibilities are endless. What will you do today to make you life better?

_____
_____

One thing I will do today that is slightly out of my comfort zone.

Those scary things that you think you can't do. What is the worst that will happen? Make that phone call, ask for that raise, create that video, do what ever it takes to pull yourself out of your comfort zone, just one small thing each day will make a huge difference.

_____
_____

Doodle of the Day

Create whatever causes a revolution in your heart. -Elizabeth Gilbert

How does this quote make you feel?

Notes

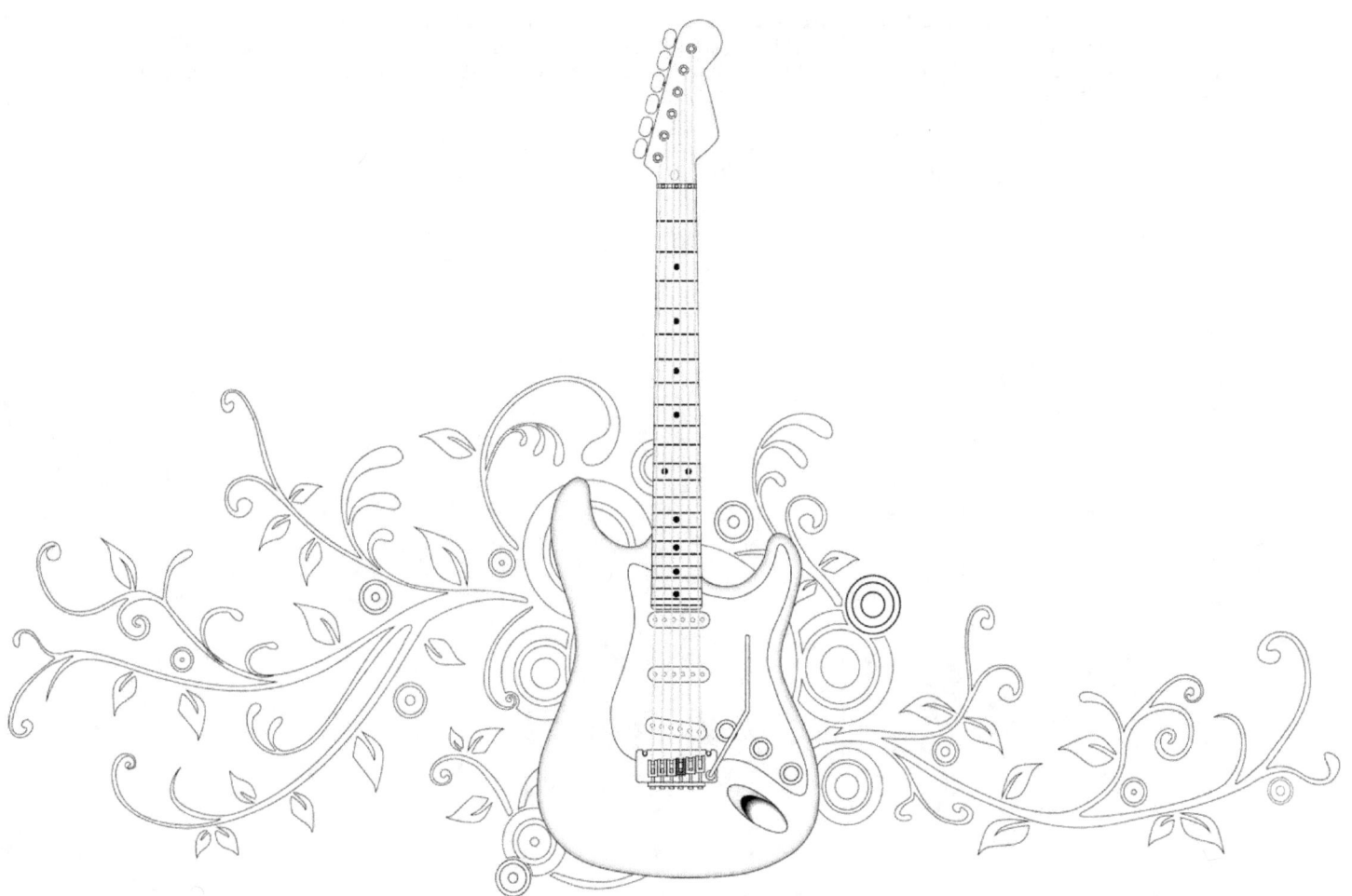

Date _____

> Any activity becomes creative when the doer cares about doing it right, or better.
> -John Updike

Today's Creative Pursuit

What creativity will I pursue today? Baking, decorating, coloring, painting, music, creating software or a spreadsheet? The possibilities are endless.

_____
_____

MORNING HABITS

What are the habits I want to build, increase or pay attention to? Sleep, water, meditation and journaling are the ones that are high on my list, what else do you want to add?

- [ ] 1. My time to get up is _____ am.
- [ ] 2. I will drink _____ glasses of water.
- [ ] 3. I did _____ minutes of Meditation.
- [ ] 4. I Journaled this morning.
- [ ] 5. _____
- [ ] 6. _____

Today's Affirmations

Today's affirmations? I am creative, I am pursuing my dreams today, I am open to possibilities. What positive, present, personal statement are you making for yourself today? Repeat it at least 3 times today.

_____
_____

One action I will take today to make myself or my life better.

Today I will try a new food, today I will go to the gym, today I will send that application, the possibilities are endless. What will you do today to make you life better?

_____
_____

One thing I will do today that is slightly out of my comfort zone.

Those scary things that you think you can't do. What is the worst that will happen? Make that phone call, ask for that raise, create that video, do what ever it takes to pull yourself out of your comfort zone, just one small thing each day will make a huge difference.

_____
_____

Doodle of the Day

Energy is the key to creativity. Energy is the key to life. -William Shatner

How does this quote make you feel?

Notes

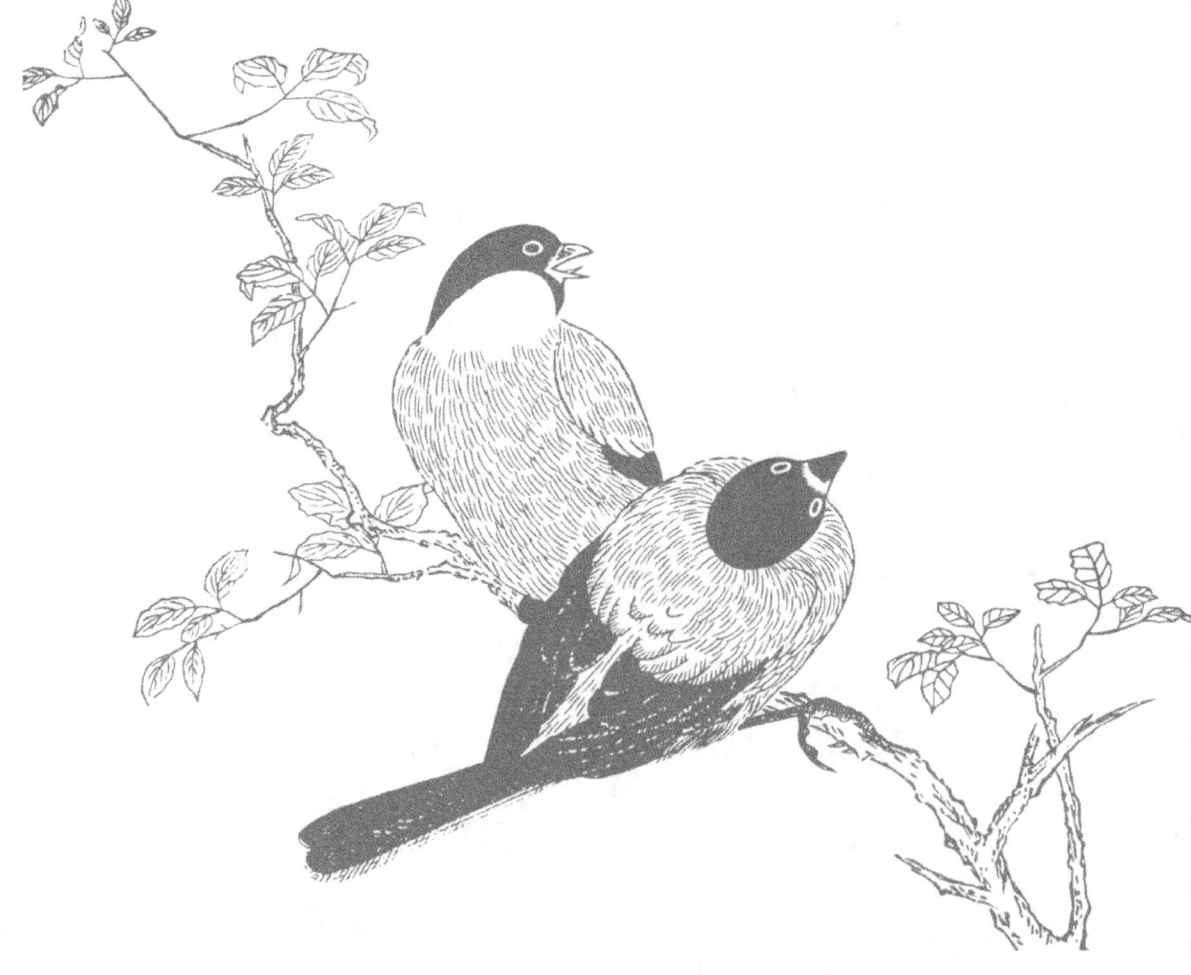

Date _____

> It was anger more than anything else that had set me off, roused me into productivity and creativity. -Mary Garden

MORNING HABITS

What are the habits I want to build, increase or pay attention to? Sleep, water , meditation and journaling are the ones that are high on my list, what else do you want to add?

- [ ] 1. My time to get up is _____ am.
- [ ] 2. I will drink _____ glasses of water.
- [ ] 3. I did _____ minutes of Meditation.
- [ ] 4. I Journaled this morning.
- [ ] 5. _____
- [ ] 6. _____

Today's Creative Pursuit

What creativity will I pursue today? Baking, decorating, coloring, painting, music, creating software or a spreadsheet? The possibilities are endless.

_____
_____
_____

Today's Affirmations

Today's affirmations? I am creative, I am pursuing my dreams today, I am open to possibilities. What positive, present, personal statement are you making for yourself today? Repeat it at least 3 times today.

_____
_____
_____

One action I will take today to make myself or my life better.

Today I will try a new food, today I will go to the gym, today I will send that application, the possibilities are endless. What will you do today to make you life better?

_____
_____

One thing I will do today that is slightly out of my comfort zone.

Those scary things that you think you can't do. What is the worst that will happen? Make that phone call, ask for that raise, create that video, do what ever it takes to pull yourself out of your comfort zone, just one small thing each day will make a huge difference.

_____
_____

Doodle of the Day

Creativity means to push open the heavy, groaning doorway to life.
-Daisaku Ikeda

How does this quote make you feel?

Notes

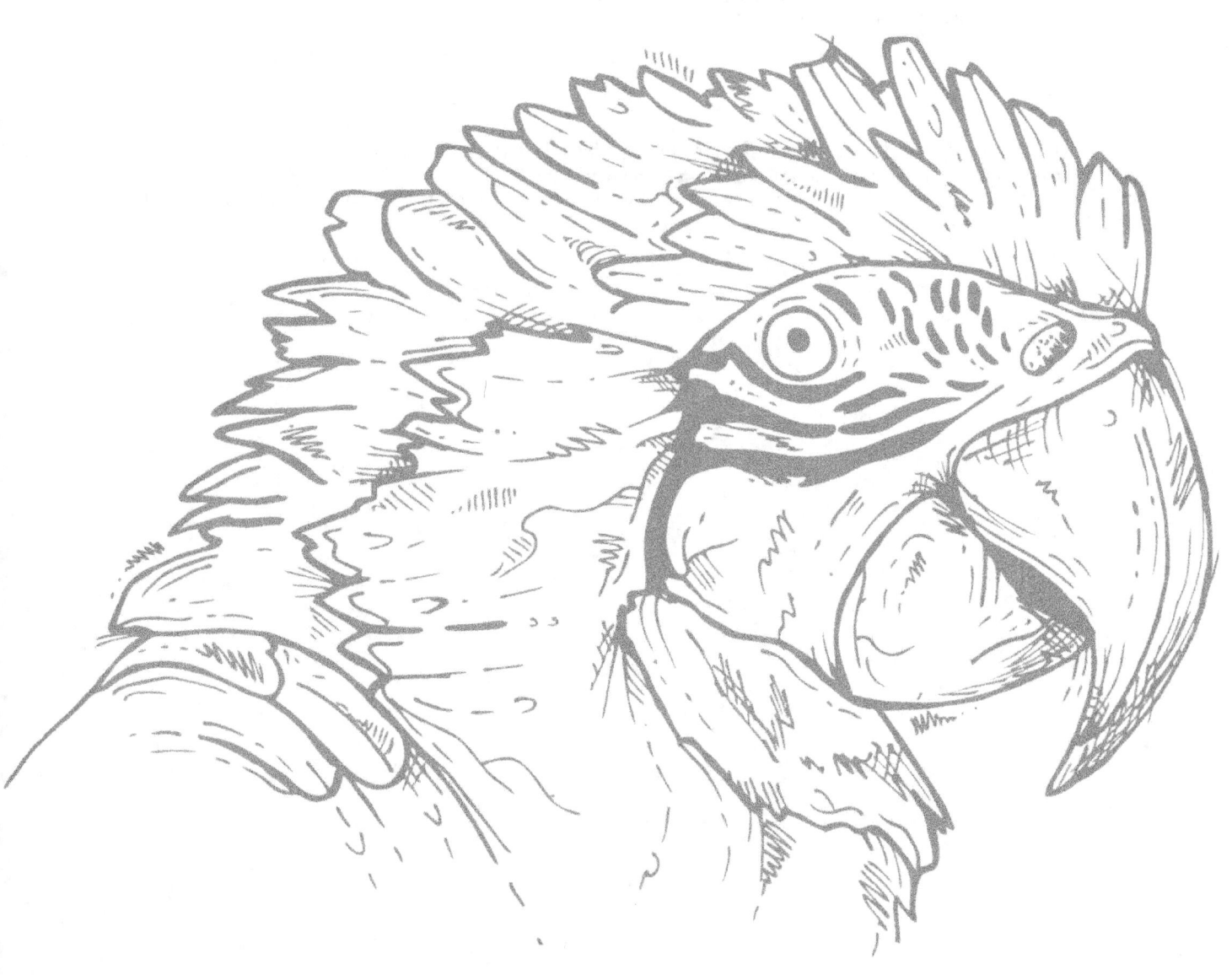

Date _____

> Creativity is the ability to introduce order
> into the randomness of nature.
> -Eric Hoffer

MORNING HABITS

What are the habits I want to build, increase or pay attention to? Sleep, water, meditation and journaling are the ones that are high on my list, what else do you want to add?

☐ 1. My time to get up is _____ am.
☐ 2. I will drink _____ glasses of water.
☐ 3. I did _____ minutes of Meditation.
☐ 4. I Journaled this morning.
☐ 5. _____
☐ 6. _____

Today's Creative Pursuit

What creativity will I pursue today? Baking, decorating, coloring, painting, music, creating software or a spreadsheet? The possibilities are endless.

_____
_____
_____

Today's Affirmations

Today's affirmations? I am creative, I am pursuing my dreams today, I am open to possibilities. What positive, present, personal statement are you making for yourself today? Repeat it at least 3 times today.

_____
_____
_____

One action I will take today to make myself or my life better.

Today I will try a new food, today I will go to the gym, today I will send that application, the possibilities are endless. What will you do today to make you life better?

_____
_____

One thing I will do today that is slightly out of my comfort zone.

Those scary things that you think you can't do. What is the worst that will happen? Make that phone call, ask for that raise, create that video, do what ever it takes to pull yourself out of your comfort zone, just one small thing each day will make a huge difference.

_____
_____

Doodle of the Day

Creativity takes courage. -Henri Matisse

How does this quote make you feel?

Notes

Date _____

> When we are angry or depressed in our creativity, we have misplaced our power.
> -Julia Margaret Cameron

MORNING HABITS

What are the habits I want to build, increase or pay attention to? Sleep, water, meditation and journaling are the ones that are high on my list, what else do you want to add?

- [ ] 1. My time to get up is _____ am.
- [ ] 2. I will drink _____ glasses of water.
- [ ] 3. I did _____ minutes of Meditation.
- [ ] 4. I Journaled this morning.
- [ ] 5. _____
- [ ] 6. _____

Today's Creative Pursuit

What creativity will I pursue today? Baking, decorating, coloring, painting, music, creating software or a spreadsheet? The possibilities are endless.

_____
_____
_____

Today's Affirmations

Today's affirmations? I am creative, I am pursuing my dreams today, I am open to possibilities. What positive, present, personal statement are you making for yourself today? Repeat it at least 3 times today.

_____
_____
_____

One action I will take today to make myself or my life better.

Today I will try a new food, today I will go to the gym, today I will send that application, the possibilities are endless. What will you do today to make you life better?

_____
_____

One thing I will do today that is slightly out of my comfort zone.

Those scary things that you think you can't do. What is the worst that will happen? Make that phone call, ask for that raise, create that video, do what ever it takes to pull yourself out of your comfort zone, just one small thing each day will make a huge difference.

_____
_____

Doodle of the Day

Creativity is a natural extension of our enthusiasm. -Earl Nightingale

How does this quote make you feel?

Notes

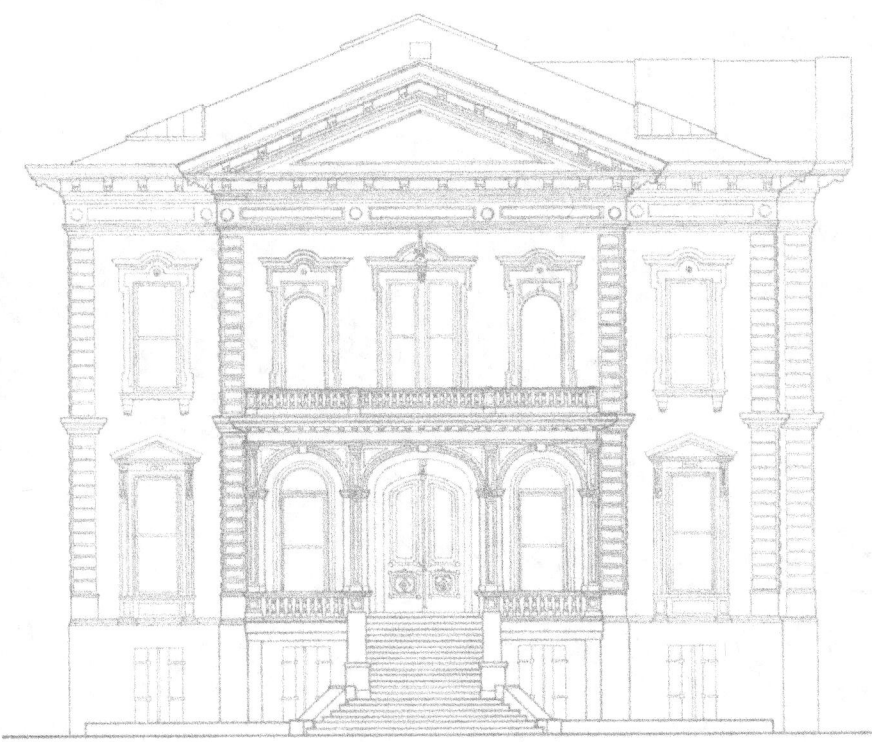

Date _____

> Creativity is a great motivator because it makes people interested in what they are doing. -Edward de Bono

Today's Creative Pursuit

What creativity will I pursue today? Baking, decorating, coloring, painting, music, creating software or a spreadsheet? The possibilities are endless.

_____
_____
_____

Today's Affirmations

Today's affirmations? I am creative, I am pursuing my dreams today, I am open to possibilities. What positive, present, personal statement are you making for yourself today? Repeat it at least 3 times today.

_____
_____
_____

MORNING HABITS

What are the habits I want to build, increase or pay attention to? Sleep, water, meditation and journaling are the ones that are high on my list, what else do you want to add?

1. My time to get up is _____ am.
2. I will drink _____ glasses of water.
3. I did _____ minutes of Meditation.
4. I Journaled this morning.
5. _____
6. _____

One action I will take today to make myself or my life better.

Today I will try a new food, today I will go to the gym, today I will send that application, the possibilities are endless. What will you do today to make you life better?

_____
_____

One thing I will do today that is slightly out of my comfort zone.

Those scary things that you think you can't do. What is the worst that will happen? Make that phone call, ask for that raise, create that video, do what ever it takes to pull yourself out of your comfort zone, just one small thing each day will make a huge difference.

_____
_____

Doodle of the Day

Making the simple, awesomely simple, that's creativity. -Charles Mingus

How does this quote make you feel?

Notes

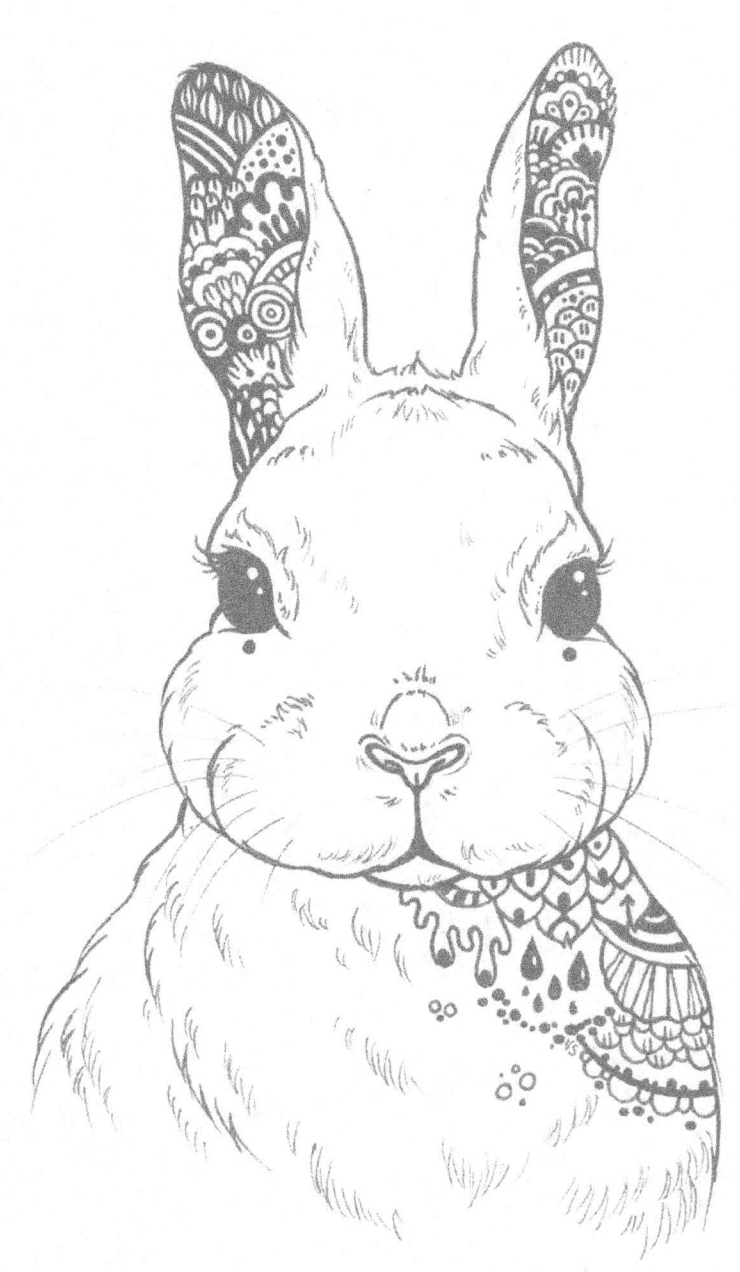

Date _____

> Let us be about setting high standards for
> life, love, creativity, and wisdom.
> -Greg Anderson

MORNING HABITS

What are the habits I want to build, increase or pay attention to? Sleep, water, meditation and journaling are the ones that are high on my list, what else do you want to add?

- ☐ 1. My time to get up is _____ am.
- ☐ 2. I will drink _____ glasses of water.
- ☐ 3. I did _____ minutes of Meditation.
- ☐ 4. I Journaled this morning.
- ☐ 5. _____
- ☐ 6. _____

Today's Creative Pursuit

What creativity will I pursue today? Baking, decorating, coloring, painting, music, creating software or a spreadsheet? The possibilities are endless.

_____
_____
_____

Today's Affirmations

Today's affirmations? I am creative, I am pursuing my dreams today, I am open to possibilities. What positive, present, personal statement are you making for yourself today? Repeat it at least 3 times today.

_____
_____
_____

One action I will take today to make myself or my life better.

Today I will try a new food, today I will go to the gym, today I will send that application, the possibilities are endless. What will you do today to make you life better?

_____
_____

One thing I will do today that is slightly out of my comfort zone.

Those scary things that you think you can't do. What is the worst that will happen? Make that phone call, ask for that raise, create that video, do what ever it takes to pull yourself out of your comfort zone, just one small thing each day will make a huge difference.

_____
_____

Doodle of the Day

Creativity comes from a conflict of ideas. -Donatella Versace

How does this quote make you feel?

Notes

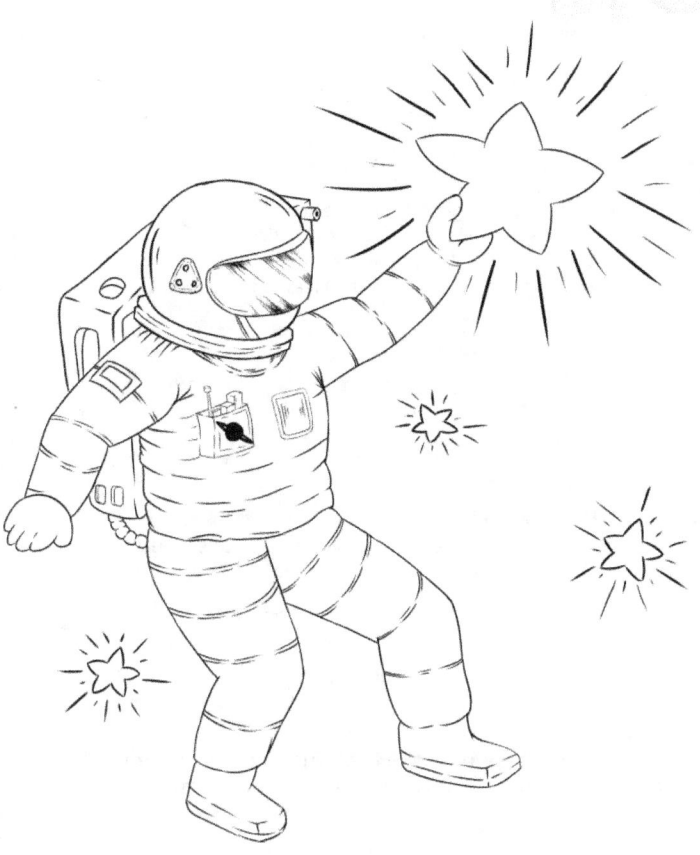

Date _____

> If you go with your instincts and keep your humor, creativity follows. With luck, success comes, too.
> -Jimmy Buffett

MORNING HABITS

What are the habits I want to build, increase or pay attention to? Sleep, water, meditation and journaling are the ones that are high on my list, what else do you want to add?

- [ ] 1. My time to get up is _____ am.
- [ ] 2. I will drink _____ glasses of water.
- [ ] 3. I did _____ minutes of Meditation.
- [ ] 4. I Journaled this morning.
- [ ] 5. _____
- [ ] 6. _____

Today's Creative Pursuit

What creativity will I pursue today? Baking, decorating, coloring, painting, music, creating software or a spreadsheet? The possibilities are endless.

_____
_____
_____

Today's Affirmations

Today's affirmations? I am creative, I am pursuing my dreams today, I am open to possibilities. What positive, present, personal statement are you making for yourself today? Repeat it at least 3 times today.

_____
_____
_____
_____

One action I will take today to make myself or my life better.
Today I will try a new food, today I will go to the gym, today I will send that application, the possibilities are endless. What will you do today to make you life better?

_____
_____

One thing I will do today that is slightly out of my comfort zone.
Those scary things that you think you can't do. What is the worst that will happen? Make that phone call, ask for that raise, create that video, do what ever it takes to pull yourself out of your comfort zone, just one small thing each day will make a huge difference.

_____
_____

Doodle of the Day

Creativity is breaking out of established patterns to look at things in a different way.
-Edward de Bono

How does this quote make you feel?

Notes

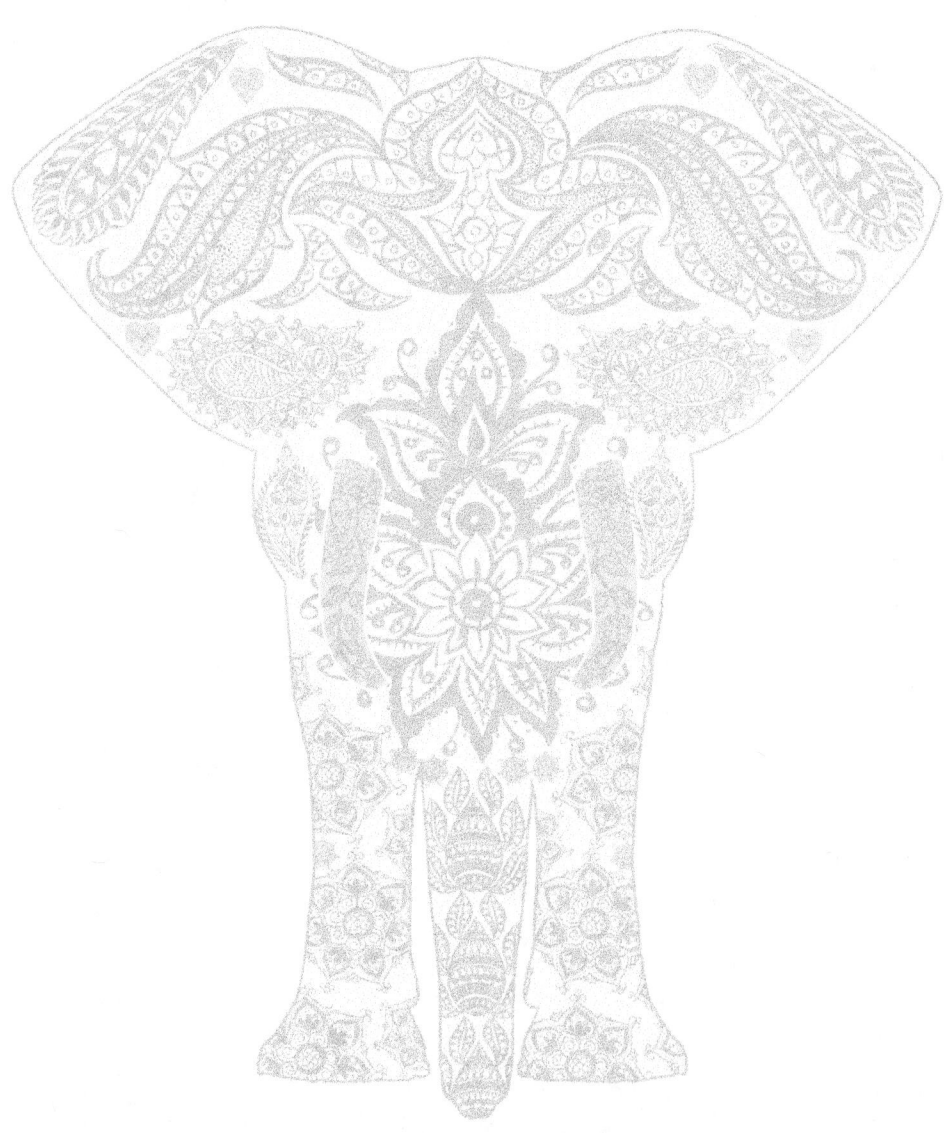

Date _____

> Enthusiasm is excitement with inspiration, motivation, and a pinch of creativity.
> -Bo Bennett

MORNING HABITS

What are the habits I want to build, increase or pay attention to? Sleep, water, meditation and journaling are the ones that are high on my list, what else do you want to add?

1. My time to get up is _____ am.
2. I will drink _____ glasses of water.
3. I did _____ minutes of Meditation.
4. I Journaled this morning.
5. _____
6. _____

Today's Creative Pursuit

What creativity will I pursue today? Baking, decorating, coloring, painting, music, creating software or a spreadsheet? The possibilities are endless.

_____
_____
_____

Today's Affirmations

Today's affirmations? I am creative, I am pursuing my dreams today, I am open to possibilities. What positive, present, personal statement are you making for yourself today? Repeat it at least 3 times today.

_____
_____
_____

One action I will take today to make myself or my life better.

Today I will try a new food, today I will go to the gym, today I will send that application, the possibilities are endless. What will you do today to make you life better?

_____
_____

One thing I will do today that is slightly out of my comfort zone.

Those scary things that you think you can't do. What is the worst that will happen? Make that phone call, ask for that raise, create that video, do what ever it takes to pull yourself out of your comfort zone, just one small thing each day will make a huge difference.

_____
_____

Doodle of the Day

Normal means lack of imagination, lack of creativity. -Jean Dubuffet

How does this quote make you feel?

Notes

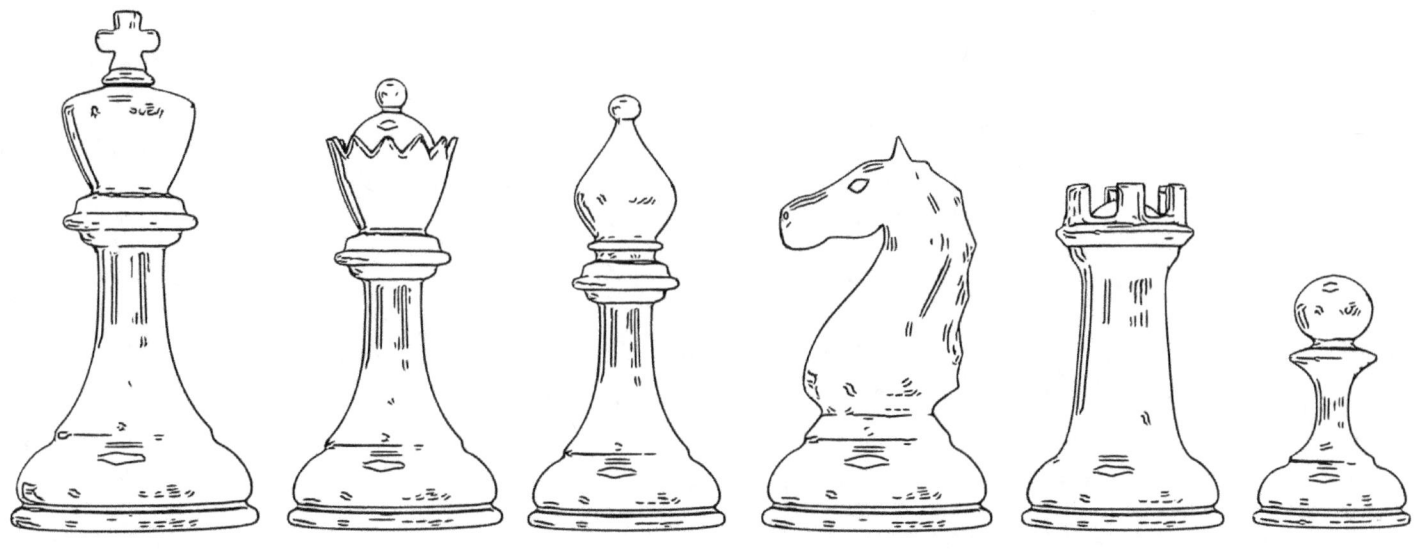

Date _____

> This simple process of focusing on things that are normally taken for granted is a powerful source of creativity.
> -Edward de Bono

MORNING HABITS

What are the habits I want to build, increase or pay attention to? Sleep, water, meditation and journaling are the ones that are high on my list, what else do you want to add?

1. My time to get up is _____ am.
2. I will drink _____ glasses of water.
3. I did _____ minutes of Meditation.
4. I Journaled this morning.
5. _____
6. _____

Today's Creative Pursuit

What creativity will I pursue today? Baking, decorating, coloring, painting, music, creating software or a spreadsheet? The possibilities are endless.

Today's Affirmations

Today's affirmations? I am creative, I am pursuing my dreams today, I am open to possibilities. What positive, present, personal statement are you making for yourself today? Repeat it at least 3 times today.

One action I will take today to make myself or my life better.

Today I will try a new food, today I will go to the gym, today I will send that application, the possibilities are endless. What will you do today to make you life better?

One thing I will do today that is slightly out of my comfort zone.

Those scary things that you think you can't do. What is the worst that will happen? Make that phone call, ask for that raise, create that video, do what ever it takes to pull yourself out of your comfort zone, just one small thing each day will make a huge difference.

Doodle of the Day

Creativity makes a leap, then looks to see where it is. -Mason Cooley

How does this quote make you feel?

Notes

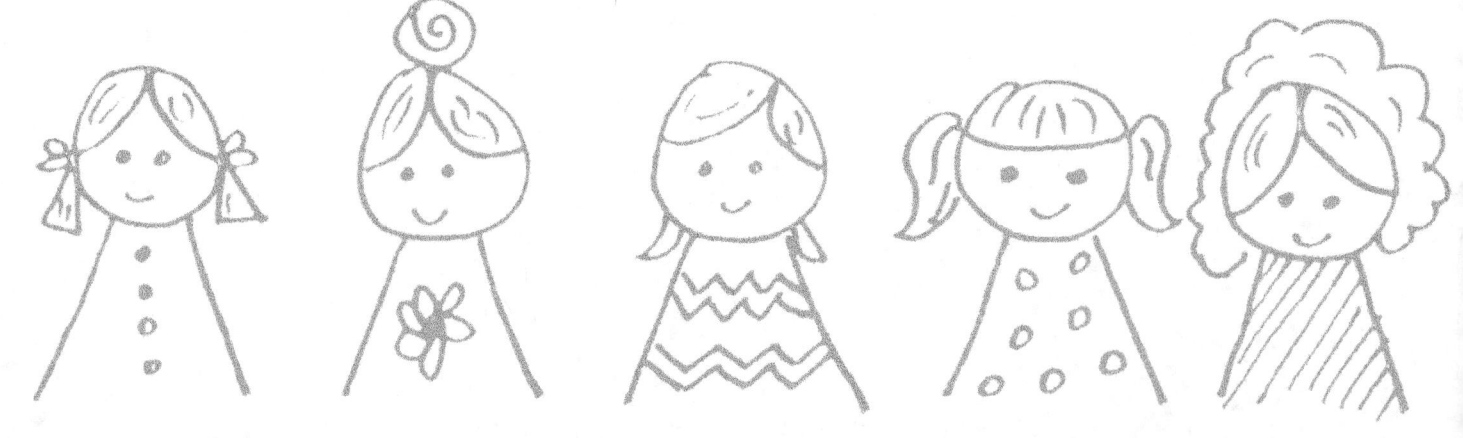

Date _____

> Creativity is not the finding of a thing, but the making something out of it after it is found. -James Russell Lowell

Today's Creative Pursuit

What creativity will I pursue today? Baking, decorating, coloring, painting, music, creating software or a spreadsheet? The possibilities are endless.

_____
_____
_____

MORNING HABITS

What are the habits I want to build, increase or pay attention to? Sleep, water, meditation and journaling are the ones that are high on my list, what else do you want to add?

☐ 1. My time to get up is _____ am.
☐ 2. I will drink _____ glasses of water.
☐ 3. I did _____ minutes of Meditation.
☐ 4. I Journaled this morning.
☐ 5. _____
☐ 6. _____

Today's Affirmations

Today's affirmations? I am creative, I am pursuing my dreams today, I am open to possibilities. What positive, present, personal statement are you making for yourself today? Repeat it at least 3 times today.

_____
_____
_____

One action I will take today to make myself or my life better.
Today I will try a new food, today I will go to the gym, today I will send that application, the possibilities are endless. What will you do today to make you life better?

_____
_____

One thing I will do today that is slightly out of my comfort zone.
Those scary things that you think you can't do. What is the worst that will happen? Make that phone call, ask for that raise, create that video, do what ever it takes to pull yourself out of your comfort zone, just one small thing each day will make a huge difference.

_____
_____

Doodle of the Day

Anxiety is the handmaiden of creativity. -T. S. Eliot

How does this quote make you feel?

Notes

Date _____

> Anxiety is part of creativity, the need to get something out. -David Duchovny

MORNING HABITS

What are the habits I want to build, increase or pay attention to? Sleep, water, meditation and journaling are the ones that are high on my list, what else do you want to add?

☐ 1. My time to get up is _____ am.
☐ 2. I will drink _____ glasses of water.
☐ 3. I did _____ minutes of Meditation.
☐ 4. I Journaled this morning.
☐ 5. _____
☐ 6. _____

Today's Creative Pursuit

What creativity will I pursue today? Baking, decorating, coloring, painting, music, creating software or a spreadsheet? The possibilities are endless.

_____
_____
_____

Today's Affirmations

Today's affirmations? I am creative, I am pursuing my dreams today, I am open to possibilities. What positive, present, personal statement are you making for yourself today? Repeat it at least 3 times today.

_____
_____
_____

One action I will take today to make myself or my life better.

Today I will try a new food, today I will go to the gym, today I will send that application, the possibilities are endless. What will you do today to make you life better?

_____
_____

One thing I will do today that is slightly out of my comfort zone.

Those scary things that you think you can't do. What is the worst that will happen? Make that phone call, ask for that raise, create that video, do what ever it takes to pull yourself out of your comfort zone, just one small thing each day will make a huge difference.

_____
_____

Doodle of the Day

An essential aspect of creativity is not being afraid to fail. -Edwin Land

How does this quote make you feel?

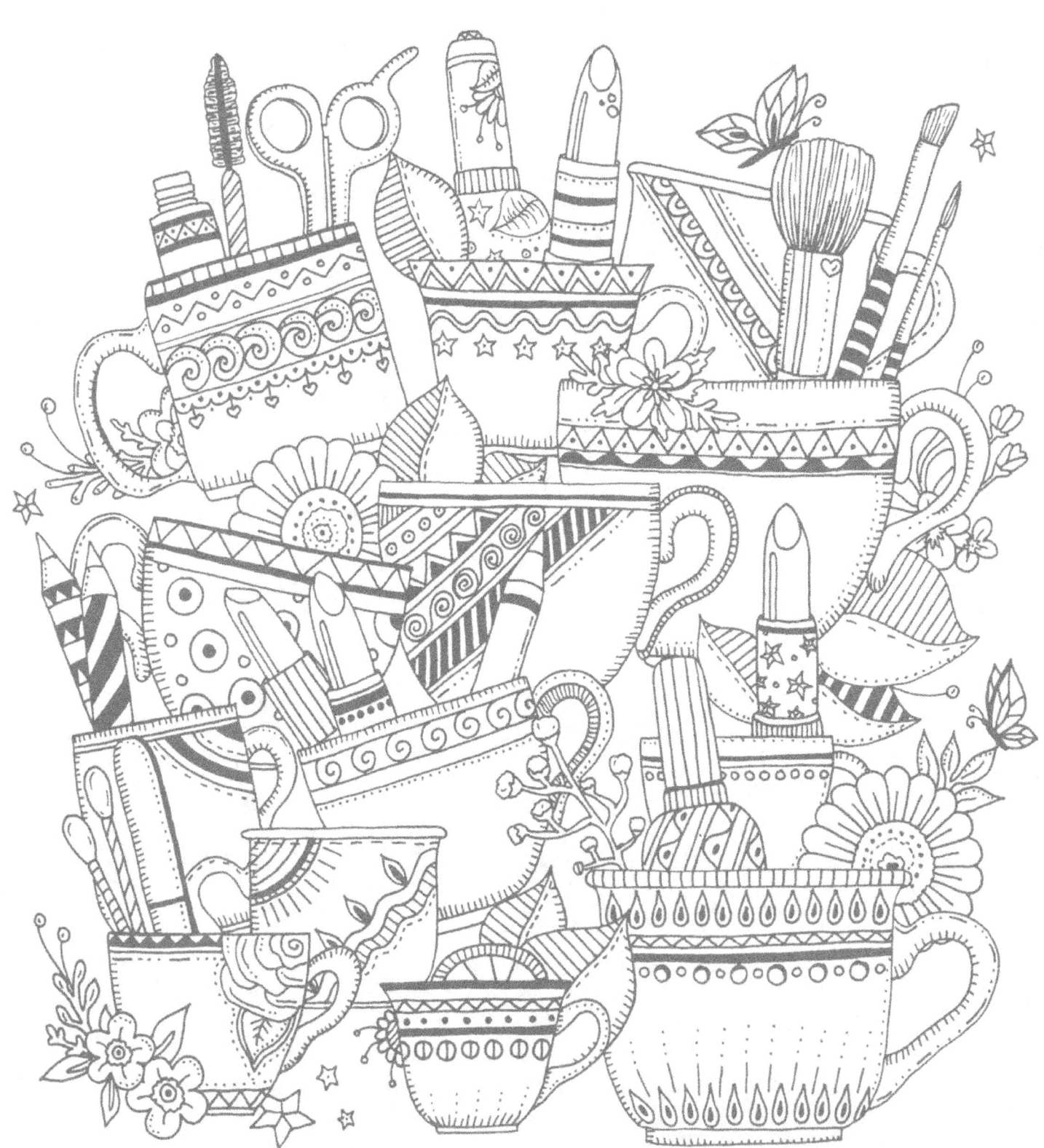

Date _____

There is a fountain of youth: it is your mind, your talents, the creativity you bring to your life. -Sophia Loren

MORNING HABITS

What are the habits I want to build, increase or pay attention to? Sleep, water, meditation and journaling are the ones that are high on my list, what else do you want to add?

☐ 1. My time to get up is _____ am.
☐ 2. I will drink _____ glasses of water.
☐ 3. I did _____ minutes of Meditation.
☐ 4. I Journaled this morning.
☐ 5. _____
☐ 6. _____

Today's Creative Pursuit

What creativity will I pursue today? Baking, decorating, coloring, painting, music, creating software or a spreadsheet? The possibilities are endless.

_____
_____
_____

Today's Affirmations

Today's affirmations? I am creative, I am pursuing my dreams today, I am open to possibilities. What positive, present, personal statement are you making for yourself today? Repeat it at least 3 times today.

_____
_____
_____

One action I will take today to make myself or my life better.

Today I will try a new food, today I will go to the gym, today I will send that application, the possibilities are endless. What will you do today to make you life better?

_____
_____

One thing I will do today that is slightly out of my comfort zone.

Those scary things that you think you can't do. What is the worst that will happen? Make that phone call, ask for that raise, create that video, do what ever it takes to pull yourself out of your comfort zone, just one small thing each day will make a huge difference.

_____
_____

Doodle of the Day

The chief enemy of creativity is good sense. -Pablo Picasso

How does this quote make you feel?

Notes

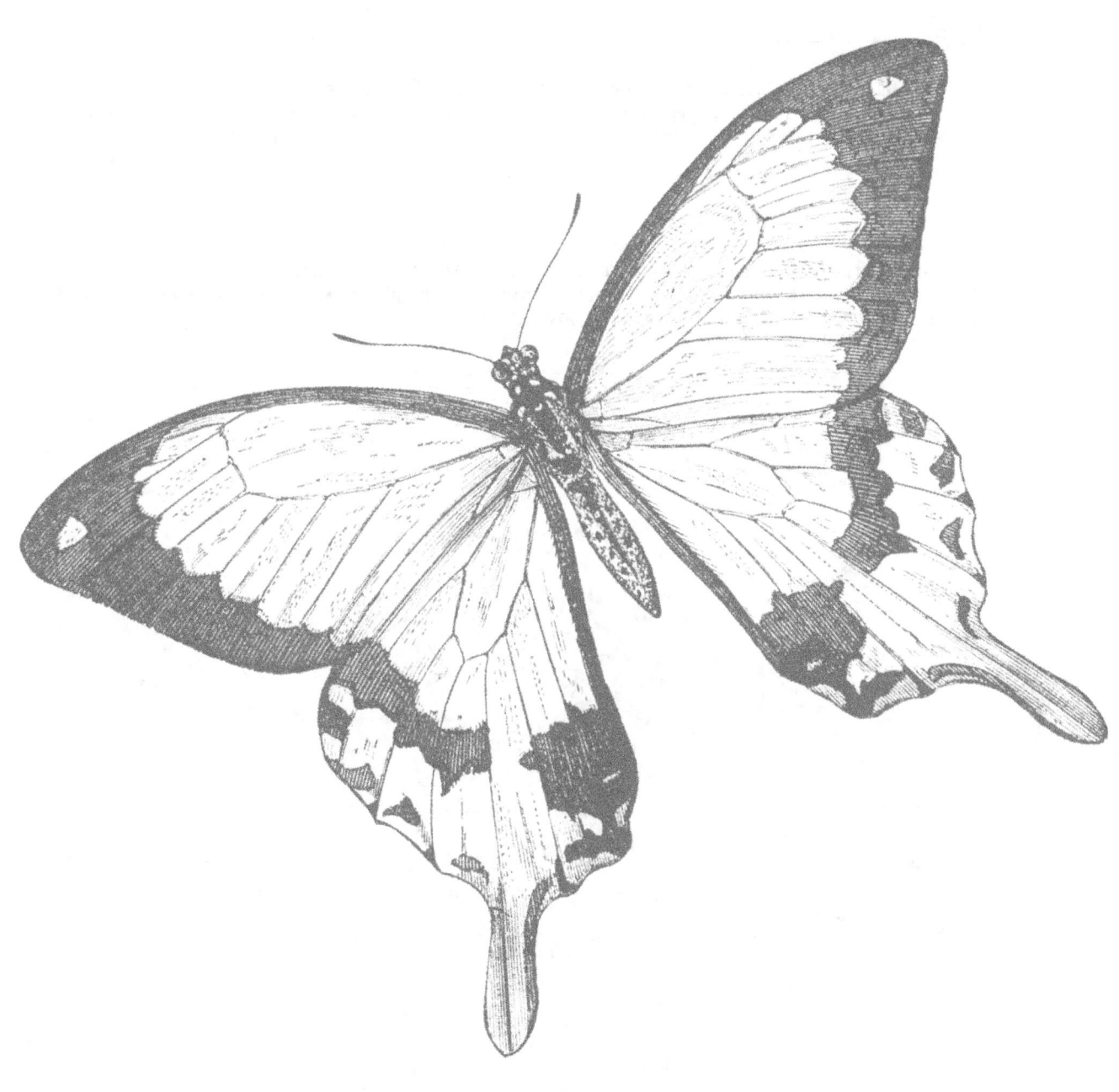

Date _____

Creativity requires the courage to let go of certainties. -Erich Fromm

MORNING HABITS

What are the habits I want to build, increase or pay attention to? Sleep, water, meditation and journaling are the ones that are high on my list, what else do you want to add?

☐ 1. My time to get up is _____ am.
☐ 2. I will drink _____ glasses of water.
☐ 3. I did _____ minutes of Meditation.
☐ 4. I Journaled this morning.
☐ 5. _____
☐ 6. _____

Today's Creative Pursuit

What creativity will I pursue today? Baking, decorating, coloring, painting, music, creating software or a spreadsheet? The possibilities are endless.

_____
_____

Today's Affirmations

Today's affirmations? I am creative, I am pursuing my dreams today, I am open to possibilities. What positive, present, personal statement are you making for yourself today? Repeat it at least 3 times today.

_____
_____

One action I will take today to make myself or my life better.

Today I will try a new food, today I will go to the gym, today I will send that application, the possibilities are endless. What will you do today to make you life better?

_____
_____

One thing I will do today that is slightly out of my comfort zone.

Those scary things that you think you can't do. What is the worst that will happen? Make that phone call, ask for that raise, create that video, do what ever it takes to pull yourself out of your comfort zone, just one small thing each day will make a huge difference.

_____
_____

Doodle of the Day

The comfort zone is the great enemy to creativity. -Dan Stevens

How does this quote make you feel?

Notes

Date _____

Creativity makes life more fun and more interesting. -Edward de Bono

MORNING HABITS

What are the habits I want to build, increase or pay attention to? Sleep, water, meditation and journaling are the ones that are high on my list, what else do you want to add?

☐ 1. My time to get up is _____ am.
☐ 2. I will drink _____ glasses of water.
☐ 3. I did _____ minutes of Meditation.
☐ 4. I Journaled this morning.
☐ 5. _____
☐ 6. _____

Today's Creative Pursuit

What creativity will I pursue today? Baking, decorating, coloring, painting, music, creating software or a spreadsheet? The possibilities are endless.

_____
_____
_____

Today's Affirmations

Today's affirmations? I am creative, I am pursuing my dreams today, I am open to possibilities. What positive, present, personal statement are you making for yourself today? Repeat it at least 3 times today.

_____
_____
_____

One action I will take today to make myself or my life better.

Today I will try a new food, today I will go to the gym, today I will send that application, the possibilities are endless. What will you do today to make you life better?

_____
_____

One thing I will do today that is slightly out of my comfort zone.

Those scary things that you think you can't do. What is the worst that will happen? Make that phone call, ask for that raise, create that video, do what ever it takes to pull yourself out of your comfort zone, just one small thing each day will make a huge difference.

_____

Doodle of the Day

The worst enemy to creativity is self-doubt. -Sylvia Plath

How does this quote make you feel?

Notes

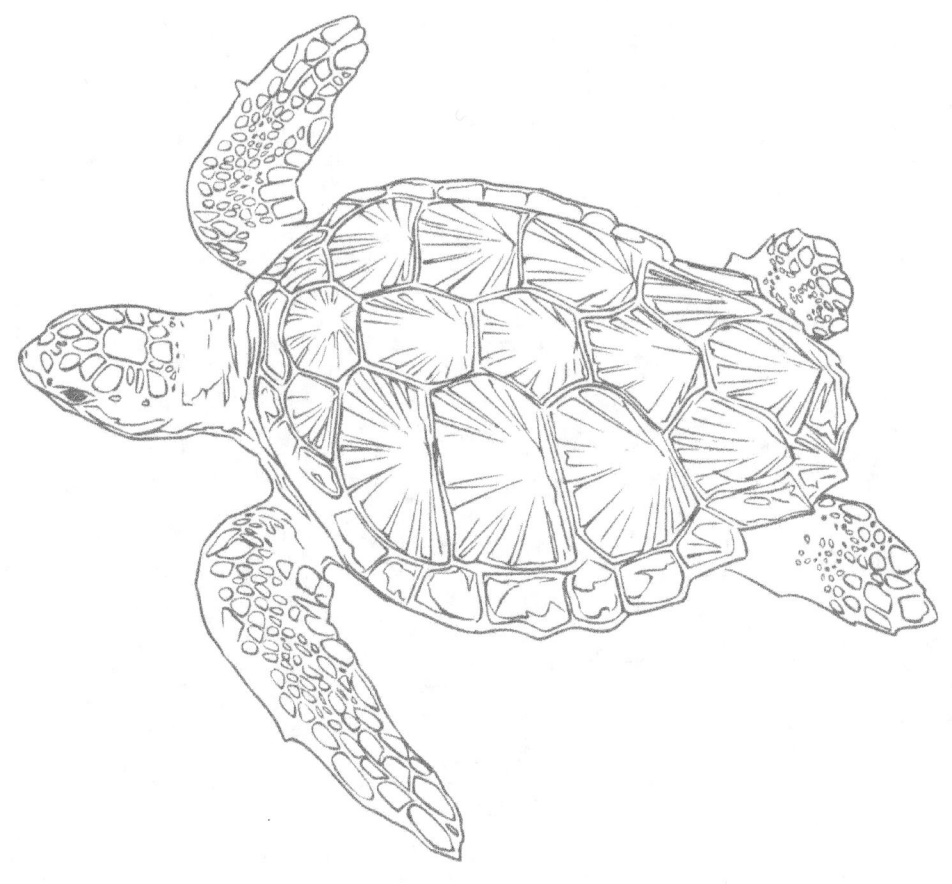

Date _____

> Creativity has got to start with humanity and when you're a human being, you feel, you suffer. -Marilyn Monroe

MORNING HABITS

What are the habits I want to build, increase or pay attention to? Sleep, water, meditation and journaling are the ones that are high on my list, what else do you want to add?

☐ 1. My time to get up is _____ am.
☐ 2. I will drink _____ glasses of water.
☐ 3. I did _____ minutes of Meditation.
☐ 4. I Journaled this morning.
☐ 5. _____
☐ 6. _____

Today's Creative Pursuit

What creativity will I pursue today? Baking, decorating, coloring, painting, music, creating software or a spreadsheet? The possibilities are endless.

_____
_____
_____

Today's Affirmations

Today's affirmations? I am creative, I am pursuing my dreams today, I am open to possibilities. What positive, present, personal statement are you making for yourself today? Repeat it at least 3 times today.

_____
_____
_____

One action I will take today to make myself or my life better.

Today I will try a new food, today I will go to the gym, today I will send that application, the possibilities are endless. What will you do today to make you life better?

_____
_____

One thing I will do today that is slightly out of my comfort zone.

Those scary things that you think you can't do. What is the worst that will happen? Make that phone call, ask for that raise, create that video, do what ever it takes to pull yourself out of your comfort zone, just one small thing each day will make a huge difference.

_____
_____

Doodle of the Day

> Don't think. Thinking is the enemy of creativity. You can't try to do things. You simply must do things. -Ray Bradbury

How does this quote make you feel?

Notes

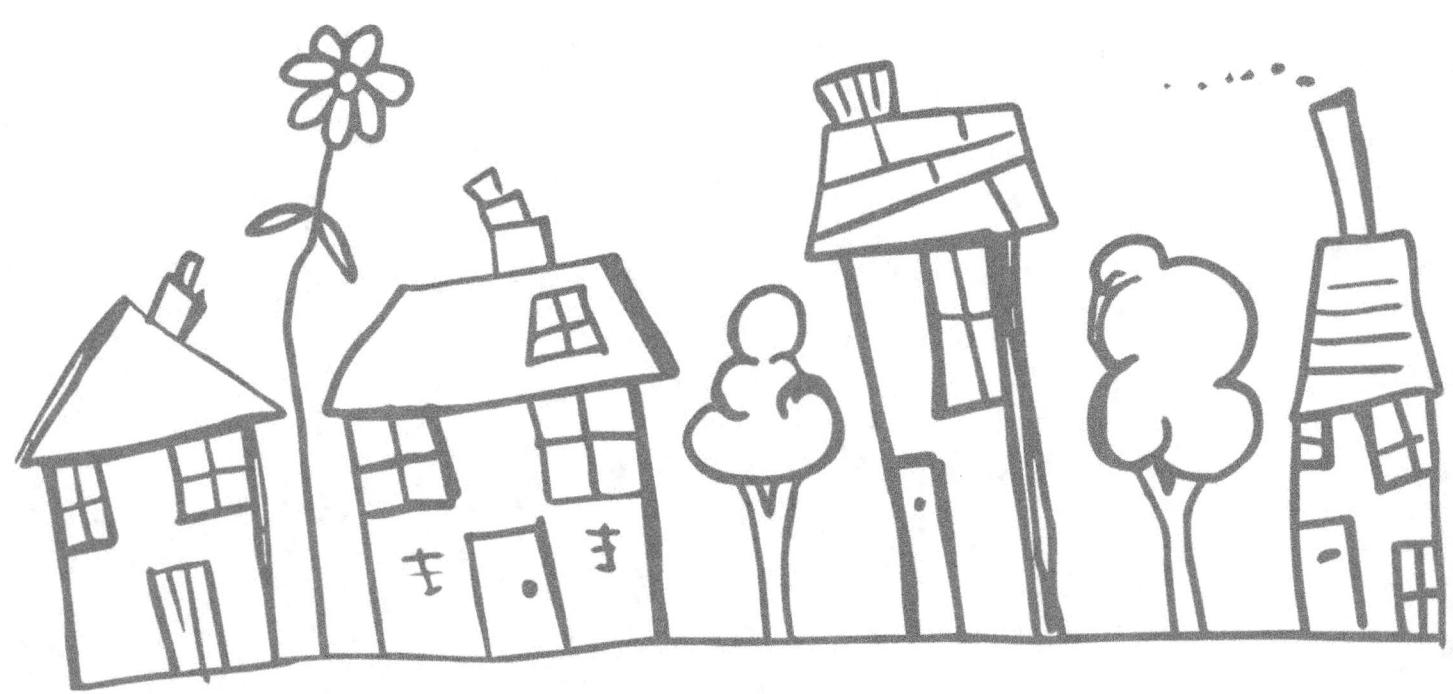

Date _____

> The most important thing is a person. A person who incites and feeds your curiosity; and machines cannot do that in the same way that people can.
> -Steve Jobs

Today's Creative Pursuit

What creativity will I pursue today? Baking, decorating, coloring, painting, music, creating software or a spreadsheet? The possibilities are endless.

_____

_____

MORNING HABITS

What are the habits I want to build, increase or pay attention to? Sleep, water, meditation and journaling are the ones that are high on my list, what else do you want to add?

☐ 1. My time to get up is _____ am.
☐ 2. I will drink _____ glasses of water.
☐ 3. I did _____ minutes of Meditation.
☐ 4. I Journaled this morning.
☐ 5. _____
☐ 6. _____

Today's Affirmations

Today's affirmations? I am creative, I am pursuing my dreams today, I am open to possibilities. What positive, present, personal statement are you making for yourself today? Repeat it at least 3 times today.

_____

_____

One action I will take today to make myself or my life better.

Today I will try a new food, today I will go to the gym, today I will send that application, the possibilities are endless. What will you do today to make you life better?

_____

_____

One thing I will do today that is slightly out of my comfort zone.

Those scary things that you think you can't do. What is the worst that will happen? Make that phone call, ask for that raise, create that video, do what ever it takes to pull yourself out of your comfort zone, just one small thing each day will make a huge difference.

_____

Doodle of the Day

Invest time in yourself to have great experiences that are going to enrich you.
-Steve Jobs

How does this quote make you feel?

Notes

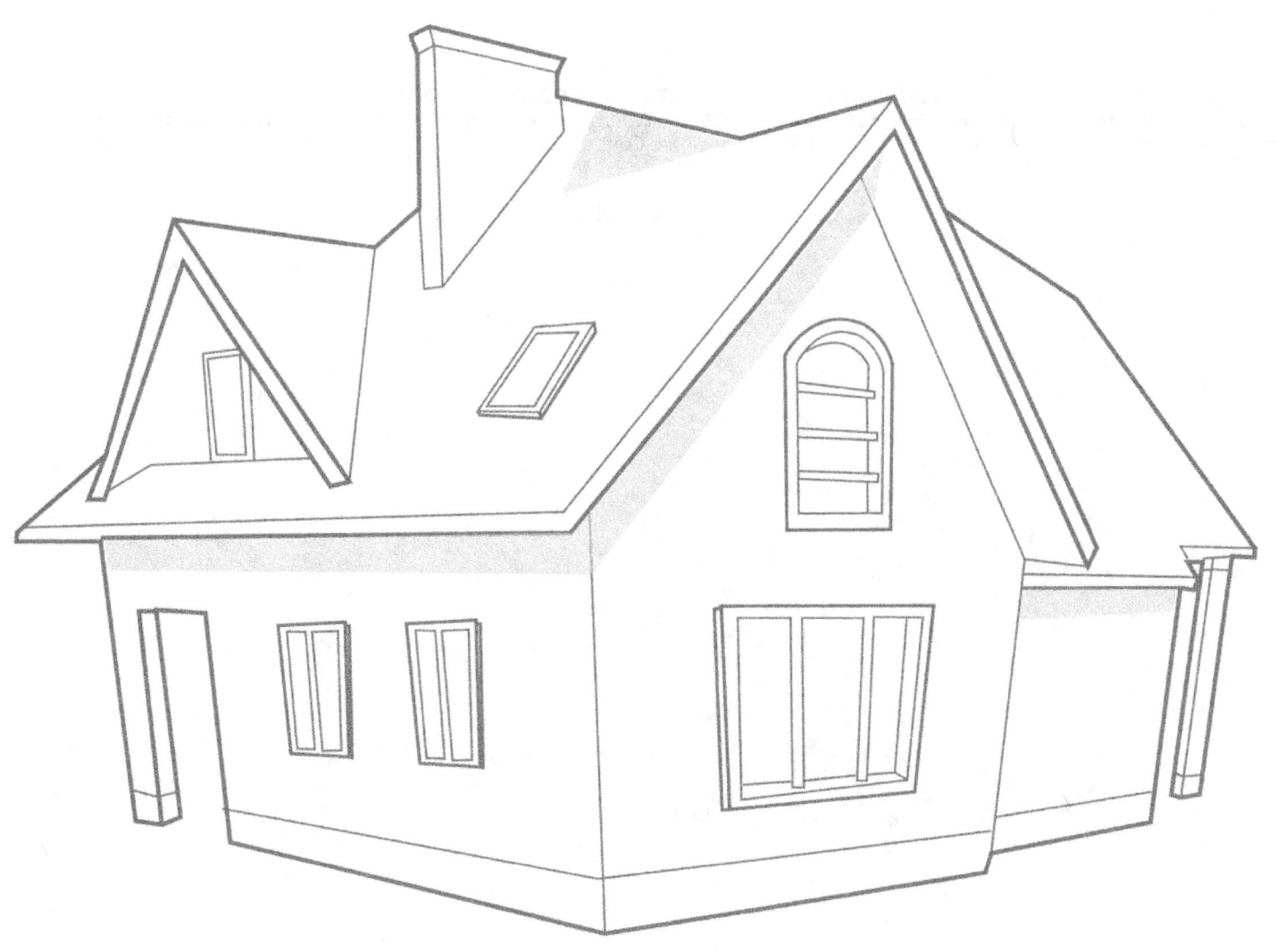

Date _____

> If today were the last of your life, would you do what you were going to do today?
> -Steve Jobs

MORNING HABITS

What are the habits I want to build, increase or pay attention to? Sleep, water, meditation and journaling are the ones that are high on my list, what else do you want to add?

- ☐ 1. My time to get up is _____ am.
- ☐ 2. I will drink _____ glasses of water.
- ☐ 3. I did _____ minutes of Meditation.
- ☐ 4. I Journaled this morning.
- ☐ 5. _____
- ☐ 6. _____

Today's Creative Pursuit

What creativity will I pursue today? Baking, decorating, coloring, painting, music, creating software or a spreadsheet? The possibilities are endless.

_____
_____
_____

Today's Affirmations

Today's affirmations? I am creative, I am pursuing my dreams today, I am open to possibilities. What positive, present, personal statement are you making for yourself today? Repeat it at least 3 times today.

_____
_____
_____

One action I will take today to make myself or my life better.

Today I will try a new food, today I will go to the gym, today I will send that application, the possibilities are endless. What will you do today to make you life better?

_____
_____

One thing I will do today that is slightly out of my comfort zone.

Those scary things that you think you can't do. What is the worst that will happen? Make that phone call, ask for that raise, create that video, do what ever it takes to pull yourself out of your comfort zone, just one small thing each day will make a huge difference.

_____
_____

Doodle of the Day

Don't let the noise of other's opinions drown out your own inner voice.
-Steve Jobs

How does this quote make you feel?

Notes

Date _____

> Learn from yesterday, live for today, hope for tomorrow. The important thing is to not stop questioning.   -Albert Einstein

MORNING HABITS

What are the habits I want to build, increase or pay attention to? Sleep, water, meditation and journaling are the ones that are high on my list, what else do you want to add?

- [ ] 1. My time to get up is _____ am.
- [ ] 2. I will drink _____ glasses of water.
- [ ] 3. I did _____ minutes of Meditation.
- [ ] 4. I Journaled this morning.
- [ ] 5. _____
- [ ] 6. _____

Today's Creative Pursuit

What creativity will I pursue today? Baking, decorating, coloring, painting, music, creating software or a spreadsheet? The possibilities are endless.

_____
_____
_____

Today's Affirmations

Today's affirmations? I am creative, I am pursuing my dreams today, I am open to possibilities. What positive, present, personal statement are you making for yourself today? Repeat it at least 3 times today.

_____
_____
_____

One action I will take today to make myself or my life better.

Today I will try a new food, today I will go to the gym, today I will send that application, the possibilities are endless. What will you do today to make you life better?

_____
_____

One thing I will do today that is slightly out of my comfort zone.

Those scary things that you think you can't do. What is the worst that will happen? Make that phone call, ask for that raise, create that video, do what ever it takes to pull yourself out of your comfort zone, just one small thing each day will make a huge difference.

_____
_____

Doodle of the Day

Creativity is contagious, pass it on. -Albert Einstein

How does this quote make you feel?

Notes

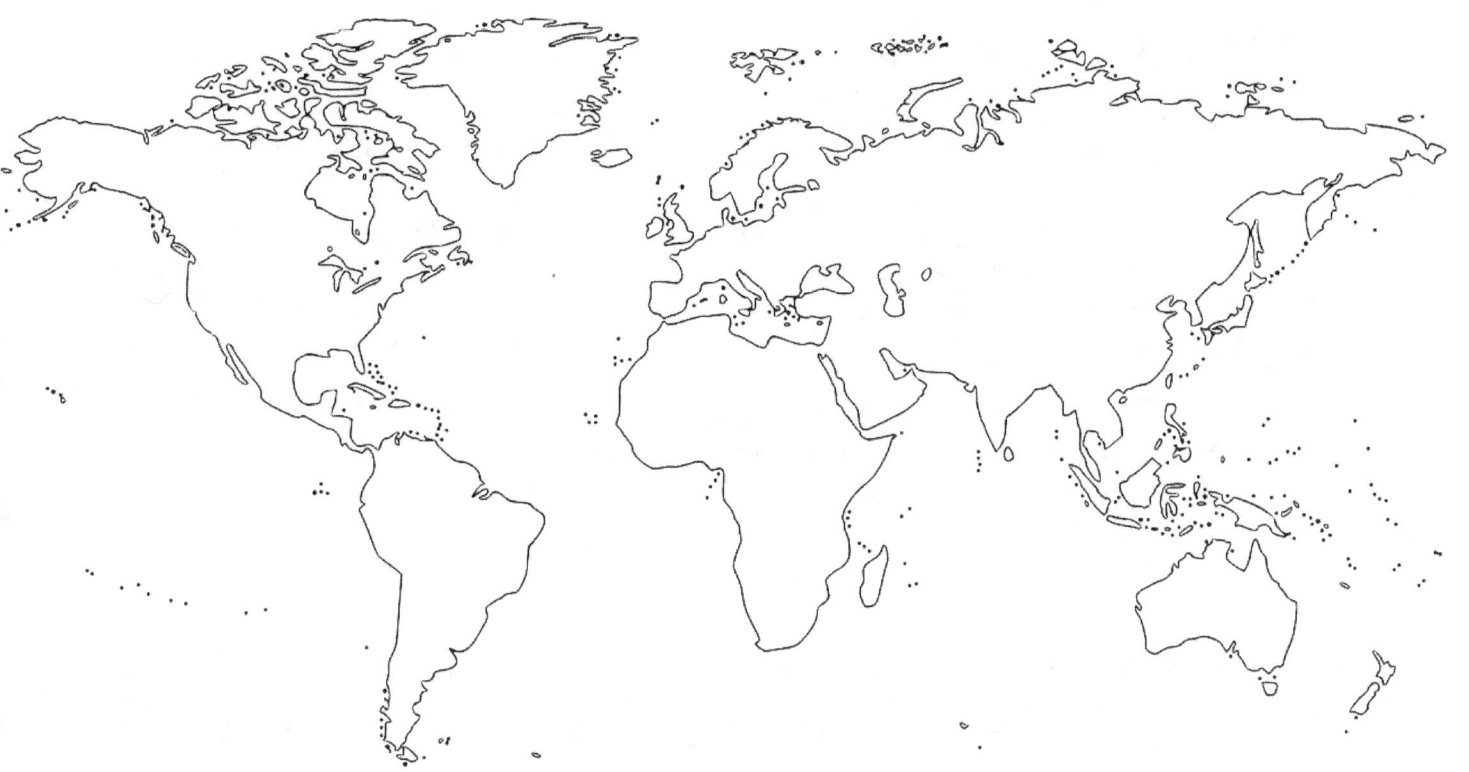

Date _____

Creativity is knowing how to hide your sources. -C.E.M. Joad

MORNING HABITS

What are the habits I want to build, increase or pay attention to? Sleep, water, meditation and journaling are the ones that are high on my list, what else do you want to add?

- ☐ 1. My time to get up is _____ am.
- ☐ 2. I will drink _____ glasses of water.
- ☐ 3. I did _____ minutes of Meditation.
- ☐ 4. I Journaled this morning.
- ☐ 5. _____
- ☐ 6. _____

Today's Creative Pursuit

What creativity will I pursue today? Baking, decorating, coloring, painting, music, creating software or a spreadsheet? The possibilities are endless.

_____
_____
_____

Today's Affirmations

Today's affirmations? I am creative, I am pursuing my dreams today, I am open to possibilities. What positive, present, personal statement are you making for yourself today? Repeat it at least 3 times today.

_____
_____
_____

One action I will take today to make myself or my life better.

Today I will try a new food, today I will go to the gym, today I will send that application, the possibilities are endless. What will you do today to make you life better?

_____
_____

One thing I will do today that is slightly out of my comfort zone.

Those scary things that you think you can't do. What is the worst that will happen? Make that phone call, ask for that raise, create that video, do what ever it takes to pull yourself out of your comfort zone, just one small thing each day will make a huge difference.

_____
_____

Doodle of the Day

> We have to continually be jumping off cliffs and developing our wings on the way down. -Kurt Vonnegut

How does this quote make you feel?

Notes

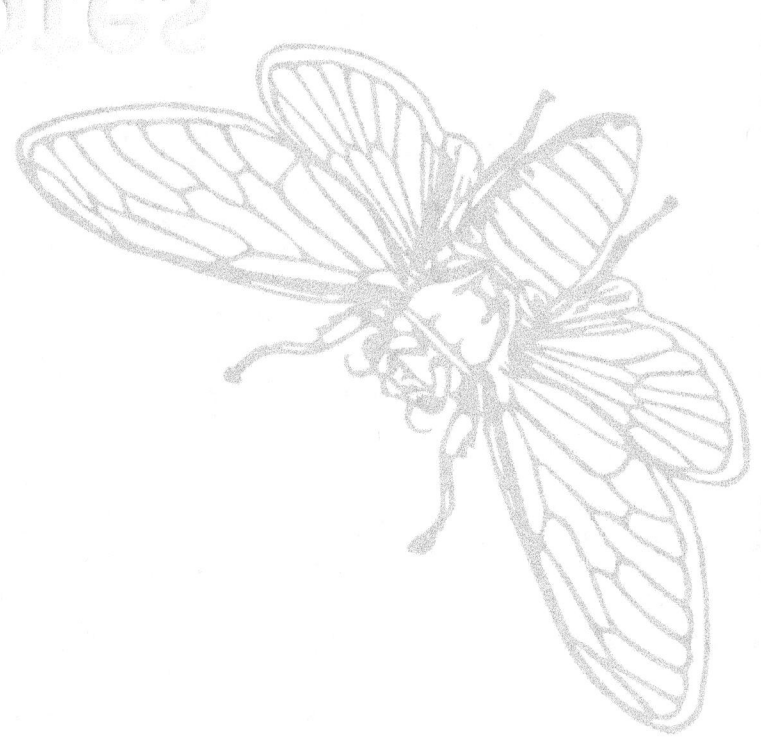

Date _____

> Others have seen what is and asked why. I have seen what could be and asked why not. -Pablo Picasso

Today's Creative Pursuit

What creativity will I pursue today? Baking, decorating, coloring, painting, music, creating software or a spreadsheet? The possibilities are endless.

_____
_____
_____

MORNING HABITS

What are the habits I want to build, increase or pay attention to? Sleep, water, meditation and journaling are the ones that are high on my list, what else do you want to add?

☐ 1. My time to get up is _____ am.
☐ 2. I will drink _____ glasses of water.
☐ 3. I did _____ minutes of Meditation.
☐ 4. I Journaled this morning.
☐ 5. _____
☐ 6. _____

Today's Affirmations

Today's affirmations? I am creative, I am pursuing my dreams today, I am open to possibilities. What positive, present, personal statement are you making for yourself today? Repeat it at least 3 times today.

_____
_____
_____

One action I will take today to make myself or my life better.

Today I will try a new food, today I will go to the gym, today I will send that application, the possibilities are endless. What will you do today to make you life better?

_____
_____

One thing I will do today that is slightly out of my comfort zone.

Those scary things that you think you can't do. What is the worst that will happen? Make that phone call, ask for that raise, create that video, do what ever it takes to pull yourself out of your comfort zone, just one small thing each day will make a huge difference.

_____
_____

Doodle of the Day

Imagination is everything. It is the preview of life's coming attractions.
-Albert Einstein

How does this quote make you feel?

Notes

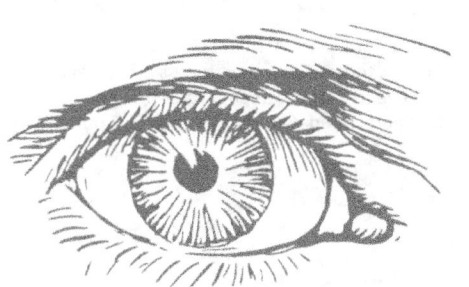
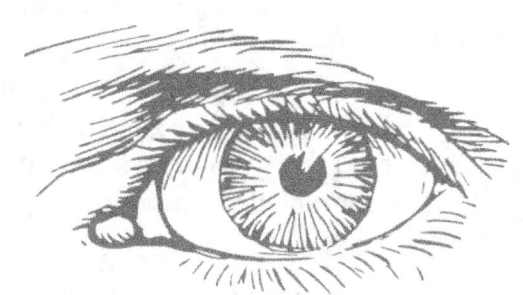

Date _____

> Doors are for people with no imagination.
> -Derek Landy

MORNING HABITS

What are the habits I want to build, increase or pay attention to? Sleep, water, meditation and journaling are the ones that are high on my list, what else do you want to add?

☐ 1. My time to get up is _____ am.
☐ 2. I will drink _____ glasses of water.
☐ 3. I did _____ minutes of Meditation.
☐ 4. I Journaled this morning.
☐ 5. _____
☐ 6. _____

Today's Creative Pursuit

What creativity will I pursue today? Baking, decorating, coloring, painting, music, creating software or a spreadsheet? The possibilities are endless.

_____
_____
_____

Today's Affirmations

Today's affirmations? I am creative, I am pursuing my dreams today, I am open to possibilities. What positive, present, personal statement are you making for yourself today? Repeat it at least 3 times today.

_____
_____
_____

One action I will take today to make myself or my life better.

Today I will try a new food, today I will go to the gym, today I will send that application, the possibilities are endless. What will you do today to make you life better?

_____
_____

One thing I will do today that is slightly out of my comfort zone.

Those scary things that you think you can't do. What is the worst that will happen? Make that phone call, ask for that raise, create that video, do what ever it takes to pull yourself out of your comfort zone, just one small thing each day will make a huge difference.

_____

Doodle of the Day

You can never solve a problem on the level on which it was created.
-Albert Einstein

How does this quote make you feel?

Notes

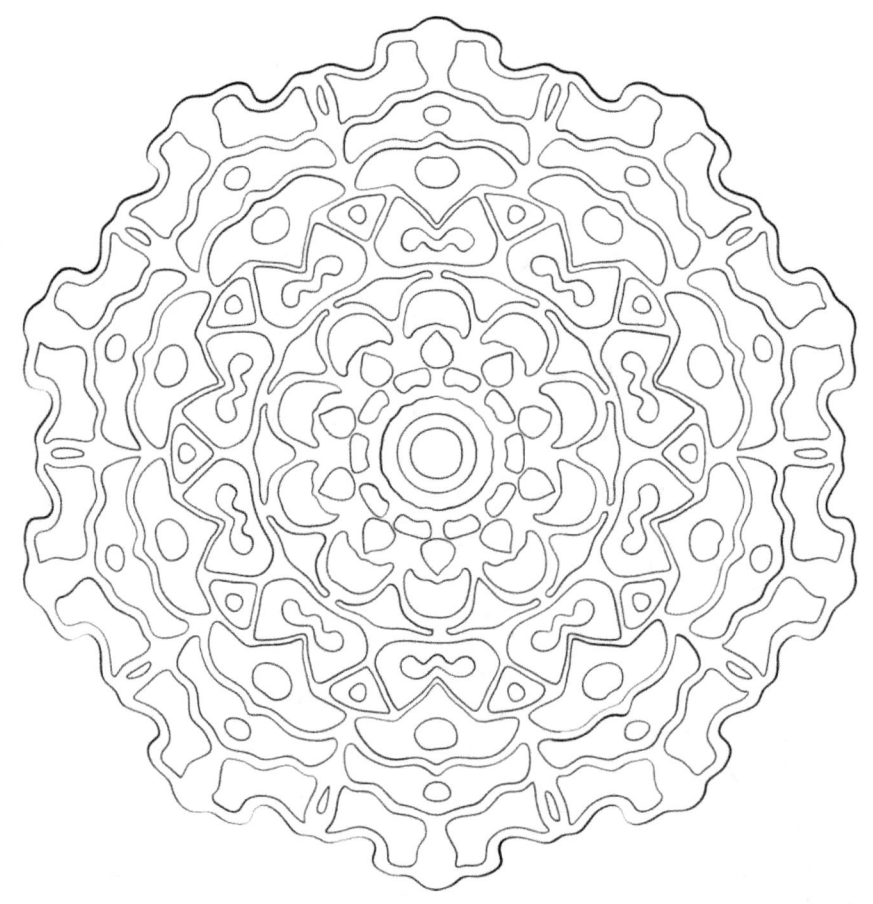

Date _____

> Vulnerability is the birthplace of innovation, creativity and change.
> -Brene Brown

MORNING HABITS

What are the habits I want to build, increase or pay attention to? Sleep, water, meditation and journaling are the ones that are high on my list, what else do you want to add?

- [ ] 1. My time to get up is _____ am.
- [ ] 2. I will drink _____ glasses of water.
- [ ] 3. I did _____ minutes of Meditation.
- [ ] 4. I Journaled this morning.
- [ ] 5. _____
- [ ] 6. _____

Today's Creative Pursuit

What creativity will I pursue today? Baking, decorating, coloring, painting, music, creating software or a spreadsheet? The possibilities are endless.

_____
_____
_____

Today's Affirmations

Today's affirmations? I am creative, I am pursuing my dreams today, I am open to possibilities. What positive, present, personal statement are you making for yourself today? Repeat it at least 3 times today.

_____
_____
_____

One action I will take today to make myself or my life better.
Today I will try a new food, today I will go to the gym, today I will send that application, the possibilities are endless. What will you do today to make you life better?

_____
_____

One thing I will do today that is slightly out of my comfort zone.
Those scary things that you think you can't do. What is the worst that will happen? Make that phone call, ask for that raise, create that video, do what ever it takes to pull yourself out of your comfort zone, just one small thing each day will make a huge difference.

_____
_____

Doodle of the Day

The urge to destroy is also a creative urge. -Mikhail Bakunin

How does this quote make you feel?

Notes

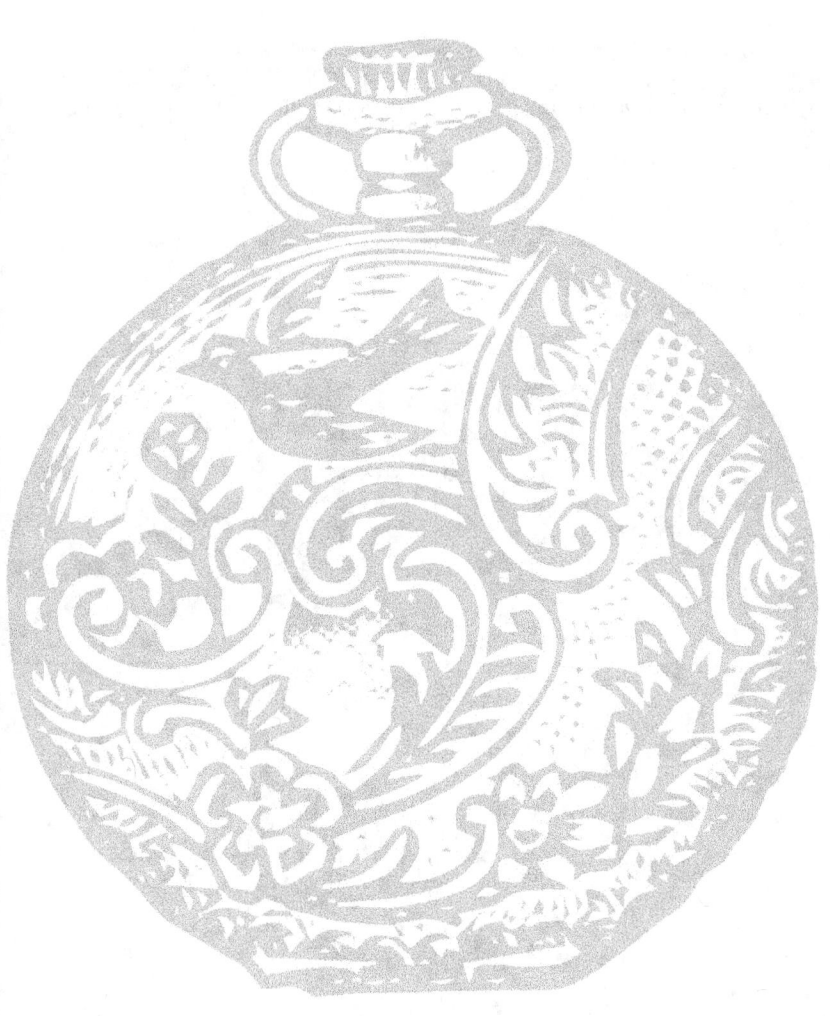

Date _____

> Everybody is talented because everybody who is human has something to express.
> -Brenda Ueland

MORNING HABITS

What are the habits I want to build, increase or pay attention to? Sleep, water, meditation and journaling are the ones that are high on my list, what else do you want to add?

☐ 1. My time to get up is _____ am.
☐ 2. I will drink _____ glasses of water.
☐ 3. I did _____ minutes of Meditation.
☐ 4. I Journaled this morning.
☐ 5. _____
☐ 6. _____

Today's Creative Pursuit

What creativity will I pursue today? Baking, decorating, coloring, painting, music, creating software or a spreadsheet? The possibilities are endless.

_____
_____
_____

Today's Affirmations

Today's affirmations? I am creative, I am pursuing my dreams today, I am open to possibilities. What positive, present, personal statement are you making for yourself today? Repeat it at least 3 times today.

_____
_____
_____
_____

One action I will take today to make myself or my life better.

Today I will try a new food, today I will go to the gym, today I will send that application, the possibilities are endless. What will you do today to make you life better?

_____
_____

One thing I will do today that is slightly out of my comfort zone.

Those scary things that you think you can't do. What is the worst that will happen? Make that phone call, ask for that raise, create that video, do what ever it takes to pull yourself out of your comfort zone, just one small thing each day will make a huge difference.

_____
_____

Doodle of the Day

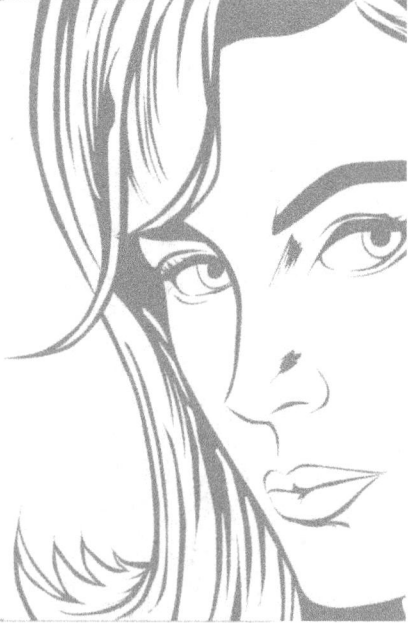

Life beats down and crushes the soul and art reminds you that you have one.
-Stella Adler

How does this quote make you feel?

Notes

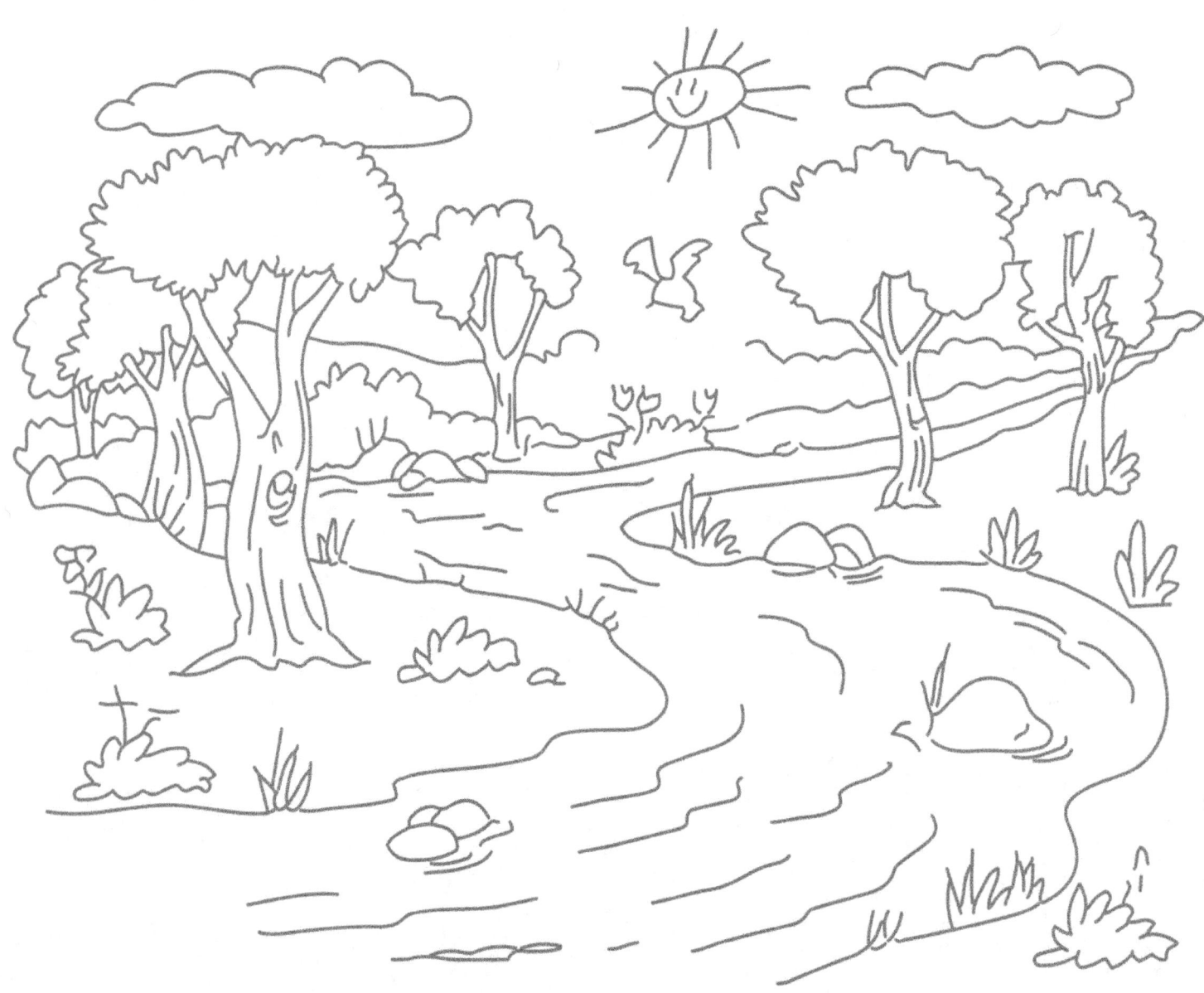

Date _____

> The true sign of intelligence is not knowledge but imagination.
> -Albert Einstein

MORNING HABITS

What are the habits I want to build, increase or pay attention to? Sleep, water, meditation and journaling are the ones that are high on my list, what else do you want to add?

- [ ] 1. My time to get up is _____ am.
- [ ] 2. I will drink _____ glasses of water.
- [ ] 3. I did _____ minutes of Meditation.
- [ ] 4. I Journaled this morning.
- [ ] 5. _____
- [ ] 6. _____

Today's Creative Pursuit

What creativity will I pursue today? Baking, decorating, coloring, painting, music, creating software or a spreadsheet? The possibilities are endless.

_____
_____
_____

Today's Affirmations

Today's affirmations? I am creative, I am pursuing my dreams today, I am open to possibilities. What positive, present, personal statement are you making for yourself today? Repeat it at least 3 times today.

_____
_____
_____

One action I will take today to make myself or my life better.

Today I will try a new food, today I will go to the gym, today I will send that application, the possibilities are endless. What will you do today to make you life better?

_____
_____

One thing I will do today that is slightly out of my comfort zone.

Those scary things that you think you can't do. What is the worst that will happen? Make that phone call, ask for that raise, create that video, do what ever it takes to pull yourself out of your comfort zone, just one small thing each day will make a huge difference.

_____
_____

Doodle of the Day

The inner fire is the most important thing mankind possesses.
-Edith Södergran

How does this quote make you feel?

Notes

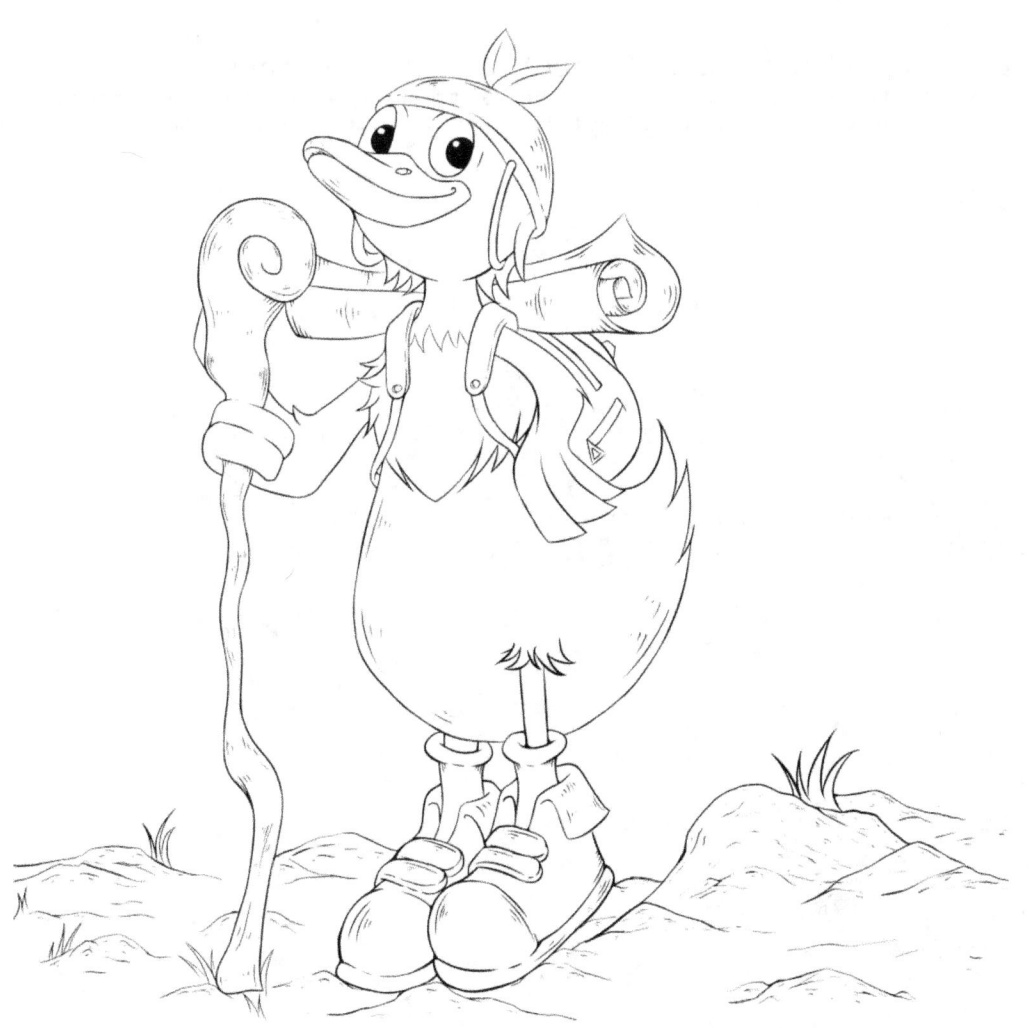

Date _____

> The road to creativity passes so close to the madhouse and often detours or ends there.
> -Ernest Becker

MORNING HABITS

What are the habits I want to build, increase or pay attention to? Sleep, water, meditation and journaling are the ones that are high on my list, what else do you want to add?

☐ 1. My time to get up is _____ am.
☐ 2. I will drink _____ glasses of water.
☐ 3. I did _____ minutes of Meditation.
☐ 4. I Journaled this morning.
☐ 5. _____
☐ 6. _____

Today's Creative Pursuit

What creativity will I pursue today? Baking, decorating, coloring, painting, music, creating software or a spreadsheet? The possibilities are endless.

_____
_____
_____

Today's Affirmations

Today's affirmations? I am creative, I am pursuing my dreams today, I am open to possibilities. What positive, present, personal statement are you making for yourself today? Repeat it at least 3 times today.

_____
_____
_____

One action I will take today to make myself or my life better.

Today I will try a new food, today I will go to the gym, today I will send that application, the possibilities are endless. What will you do today to make you life better?

_____
_____

One thing I will do today that is slightly out of my comfort zone.

Those scary things that you think you can't do. What is the worst that will happen? Make that phone call, ask for that raise, create that video, do what ever it takes to pull yourself out of your comfort zone, just one small thing each day will make a huge difference.

_____
_____

Doodle of the Day

Draw the art you want to see...– Do the work you want to see done. -Austin Kleon

How does this quote make you feel?

Notes

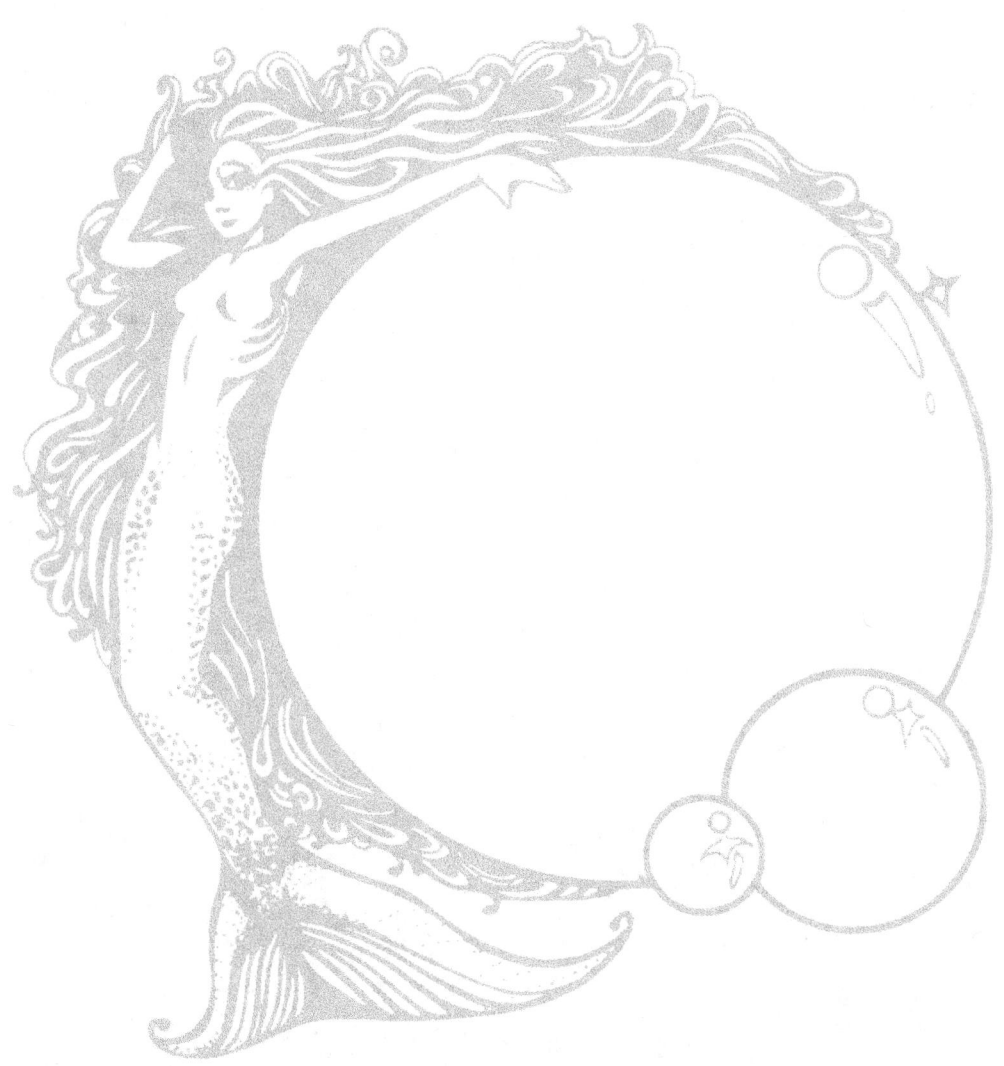

Date _____

> Our species is the only creative species,
> and it has only one creative instrument,
> the individual mind and spirit of man.
> -John Steinbeck

Today's Creative Pursuit

What creativity will I pursue today? Baking, decorating, coloring, painting, music, creating software or a spreadsheet? The possibilities are endless.

_____

_____

_____

MORNING HABITS

What are the habits I want to build, increase or pay attention to? Sleep, water, meditation and journaling are the ones that are high on my list, what else do you want to add?

- ☐ 1. My time to get up is _____ am.
- ☐ 2. I will drink _____ glasses of water.
- ☐ 3. I did _____ minutes of Meditation.
- ☐ 4. I Journaled this morning.
- ☐ 5. _____
- ☐ 6. _____

Today's Affirmations

Today's affirmations? I am creative, I am pursuing my dreams today, I am open to possibilities. What positive, present, personal statement are you making for yourself today? Repeat it at least 3 times today.

_____

_____

_____

One action I will take today to make myself or my life better.
Today I will try a new food, today I will go to the gym, today I will send that application, the possibilities are endless. What will you do today to make you life better?

_____

_____

One thing I will do today that is slightly out of my comfort zone.
Those scary things that you think you can't do. What is the worst that will happen? Make that phone call, ask for that raise, create that video, do what ever it takes to pull yourself out of your comfort zone, just one small thing each day will make a huge difference.

_____

Doodle of the Day

Everyone has their own ways of expression. I believe we all have a lot to say but finding ways to say it is more than half the battle. -Criss Jami

How does this quote make you feel?

Notes

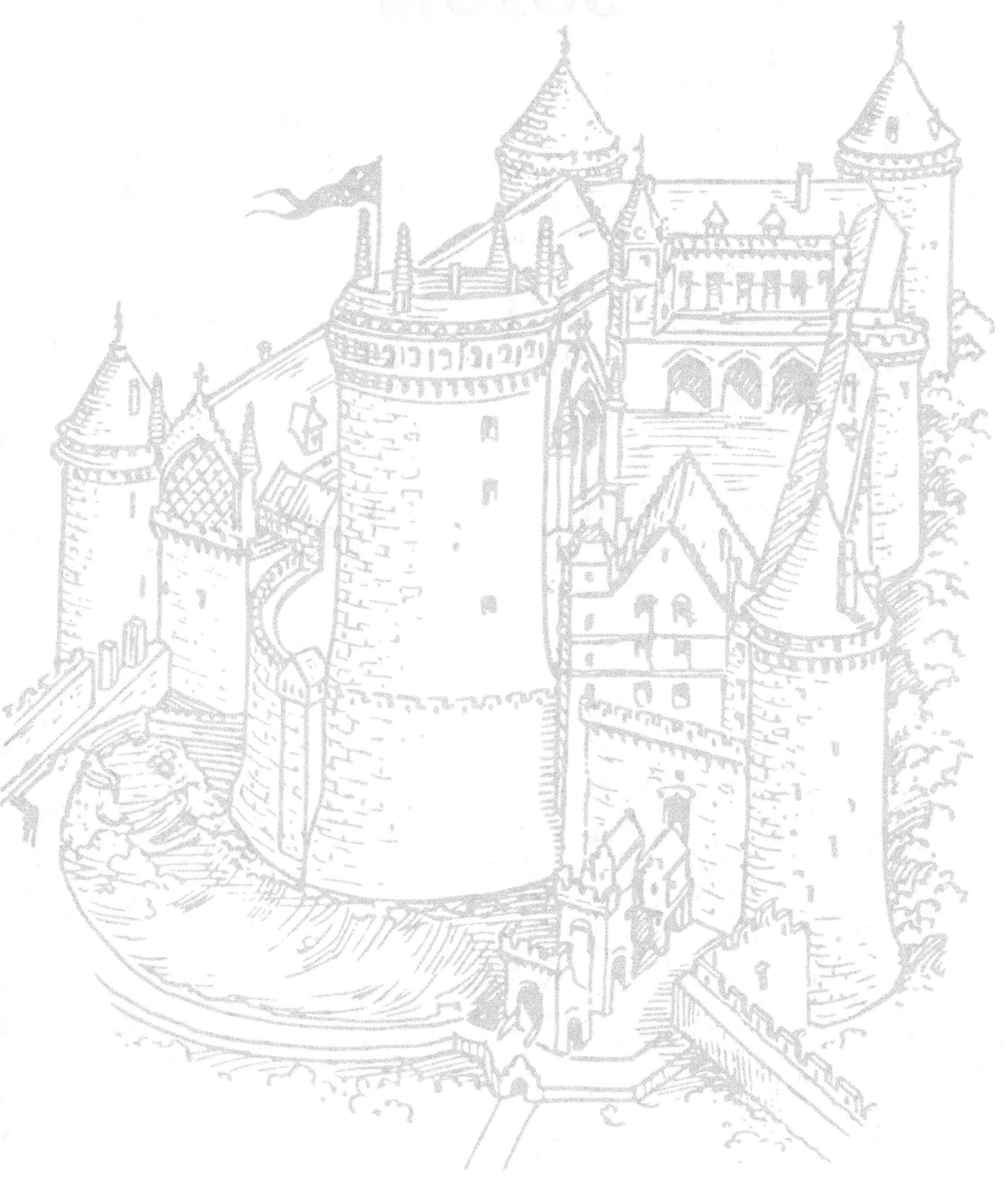

Date _____

Don't think about making art, just get it done. -Andy Warhol

Today's Creative Pursuit

What creativity will I pursue today? Baking, decorating, coloring, painting, music, creating software or a spreadsheet? The possibilities are endless.

_____
_____
_____

MORNING HABITS

What are the habits I want to build, increase or pay attention to? Sleep, water, meditation and journaling are the ones that are high on my list, what else do you want to add?

1. My time to get up is _____ am.
2. I will drink _____ glasses of water.
3. I did _____ minutes of Meditation.
4. I Journaled this morning.
5. _____
6. _____

Today's Affirmations

Today's affirmations? I am creative, I am pursuing my dreams today, I am open to possibilities. What positive, present, personal statement are you making for yourself today? Repeat it at least 3 times today.

_____
_____
_____

One action I will take today to make myself or my life better.
Today I will try a new food, today I will go to the gym, today I will send that application, the possibilities are endless. What will you do today to make you life better?

_____
_____

One thing I will do today that is slightly out of my comfort zone.
Those scary things that you think you can't do. What is the worst that will happen? Make that phone call, ask for that raise, create that video, do what ever it takes to pull yourself out of your comfort zone, just one small thing each day will make a huge difference.

_____

Doodle of the Day

Creativity is as important as literacy. -Ken Robinson

How does this quote make you feel?

Notes

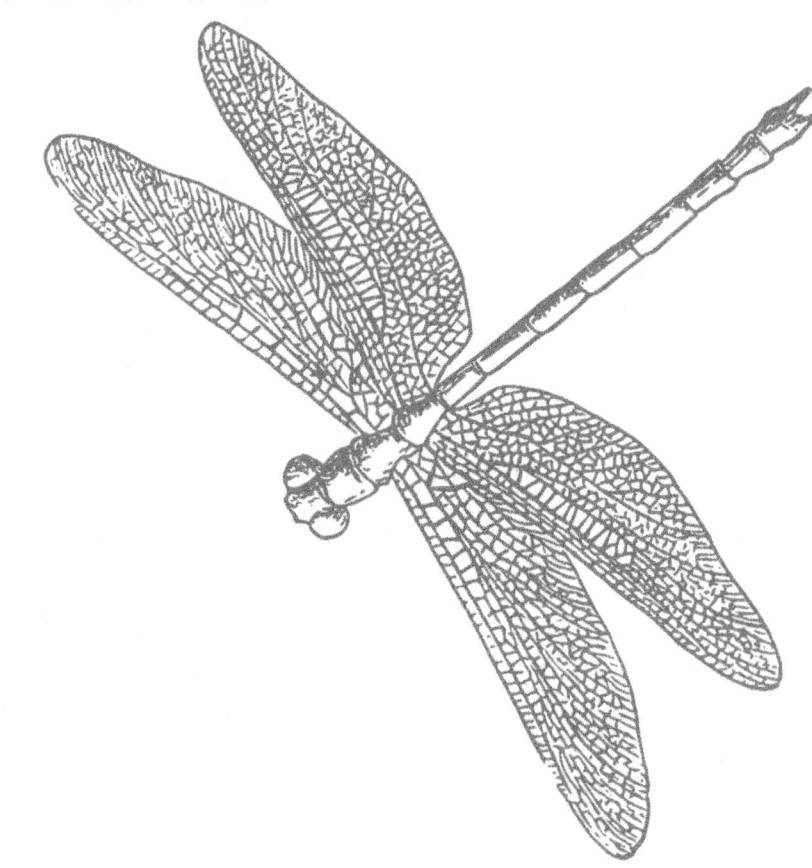

Date _____

> Imagination is the beginning of creation. You imagine what you desire, you will what you imagine and at last you create what you will. -George Bernard Shaw

MORNING HABITS

What are the habits I want to build, increase or pay attention to? Sleep, water, meditation and journaling are the ones that are high on my list, what else do you want to add?

- ☐ 1. My time to get up is _____ am.
- ☐ 2. I will drink _____ glasses of water.
- ☐ 3. I did _____ minutes of Meditation.
- ☐ 4. I Journaled this morning.
- ☐ 5. _____
- ☐ 6. _____

Today's Creative Pursuit

What creativity will I pursue today? Baking, decorating, coloring, painting, music, creating software or a spreadsheet? The possibilities are endless.

_____
_____
_____

Today's Affirmations

Today's affirmations? I am creative, I am pursuing my dreams today, I am open to possibilities. What positive, present, personal statement are you making for yourself today? Repeat it at least 3 times today.

_____
_____
_____

One action I will take today to make myself or my life better.

Today I will try a new food, today I will go to the gym, today I will send that application, the possibilities are endless. What will you do today to make you life better?

_____
_____

One thing I will do today that is slightly out of my comfort zone.

Those scary things that you think you can't do. What is the worst that will happen? Make that phone call, ask for that raise, create that video, do what ever it takes to pull yourself out of your comfort zone, just one small thing each day will make a huge difference.

_____

Doodle of the Day

Creativity is an act of defiance. -Twyla Tharp

How does this quote make you feel?

Notes

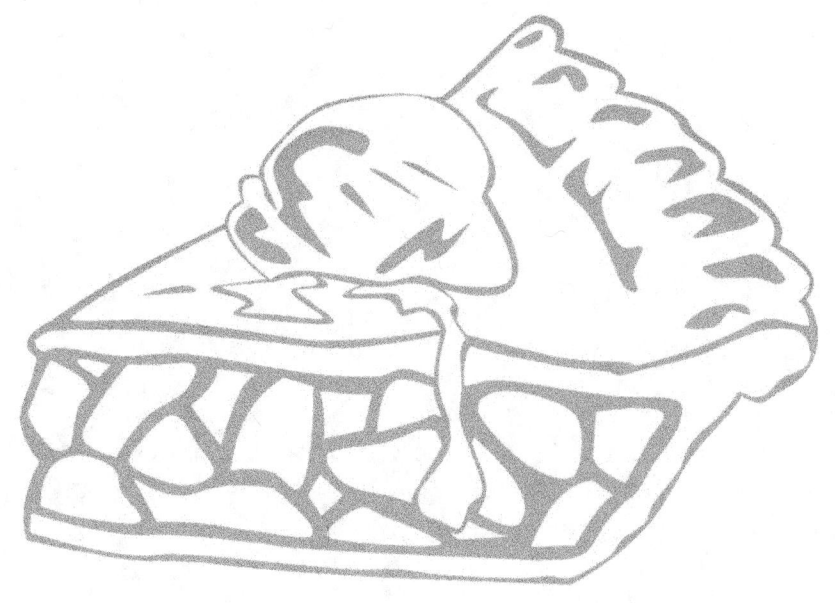

Date _____

Dance above the surface of the world. Let your thoughts lift you into creativity that is not hampered by opinion. -Red Haircrow

MORNING HABITS

What are the habits I want to build, increase or pay attention to? Sleep, water, meditation and journaling are the ones that are high on my list, what else do you want to add?

1. My time to get up is _____ am.
2. I will drink _____ glasses of water.
3. I did _____ minutes of Meditation.
4. I Journaled this morning.
5. _____
6. _____

Today's Creative Pursuit

What creativity will I pursue today? Baking, decorating, coloring, painting, music, creating software or a spreadsheet? The possibilities are endless.

_____
_____
_____

Today's Affirmations

Today's affirmations? I am creative, I am pursuing my dreams today, I am open to possibilities. What positive, present, personal statement are you making for yourself today? Repeat it at least 3 times today.

_____
_____

One action I will take today to make myself or my life better.

Today I will try a new food, today I will go to the gym, today I will send that application, the possibilities are endless. What will you do today to make you life better?

_____
_____

One thing I will do today that is slightly out of my comfort zone.

Those scary things that you think you can't do. What is the worst that will happen? Make that phone call, ask for that raise, create that video, do what ever it takes to pull yourself out of your comfort zone, just one small thing each day will make a huge difference.

_____
_____

Doodle of the Day

Create with the heart; build with the mind. -Criss Jami

How does this quote make you feel?

Notes

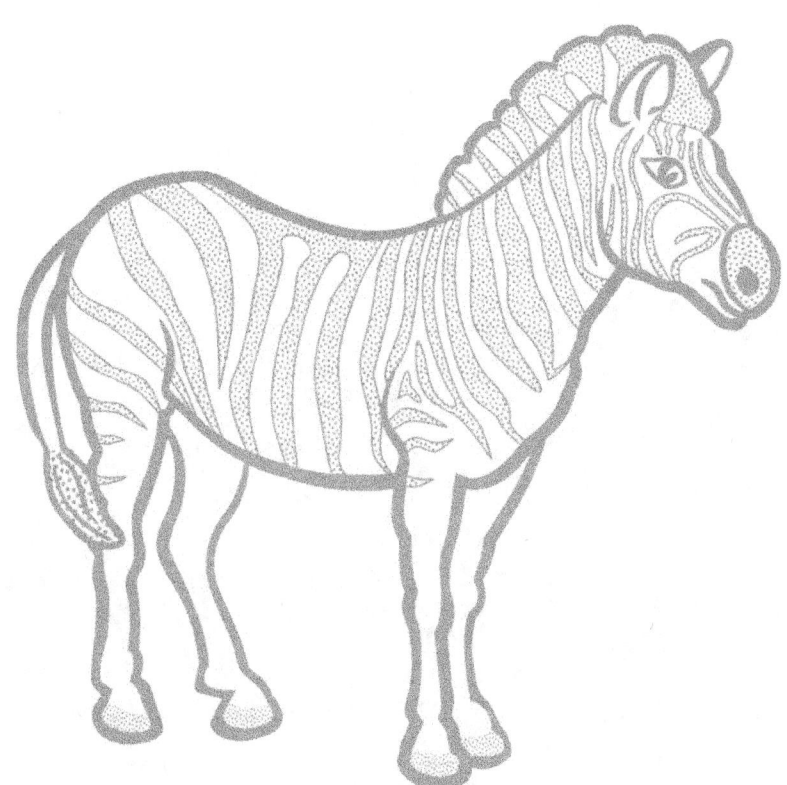

Date _____

> Art isn't only a painting. Art is anything that's creative, passionate, and personal.
> -Seth Godin

MORNING HABITS

What are the habits I want to build, increase or pay attention to? Sleep, water, meditation and journaling are the ones that are high on my list, what else do you want to add?

- [ ] 1. My time to get up is _____ am.
- [ ] 2. I will drink _____ glasses of water.
- [ ] 3. I did _____ minutes of Meditation.
- [ ] 4. I Journaled this morning.
- [ ] 5. _____
- [ ] 6. _____

Today's Creative Pursuit

What creativity will I pursue today? Baking, decorating, coloring, painting, music, creating software or a spreadsheet? The possibilities are endless.

_____
_____

Today's Affirmations

Today's affirmations? I am creative, I am pursuing my dreams today, I am open to possibilities. What positive, present, personal statement are you making for yourself today? Repeat it at least 3 times today.

_____
_____

One action I will take today to make myself or my life better.

Today I will try a new food, today I will go to the gym, today I will send that application, the possibilities are endless. What will you do today to make you life better?

_____
_____

One thing I will do today that is slightly out of my comfort zone.

Those scary things that you think you can't do. What is the worst that will happen? Make that phone call, ask for that raise, create that video, do what ever it takes to pull yourself out of your comfort zone, just one small thing each day will make a huge difference.

_____
_____

Doodle of the Day

I am my own experiment. I am my own work of art. -Madonna

How does this quote make you feel?

Notes

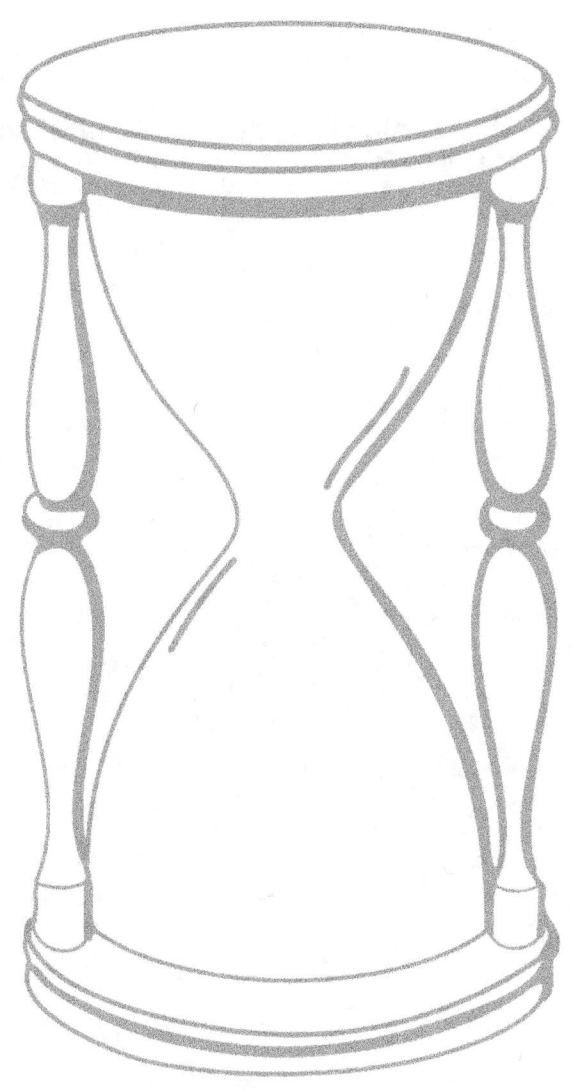

Date _____

> What keeps life fascinating is the constant creativity of the soul.
> -Deepak Chopra

Today's Creative Pursuit

What creativity will I pursue today? Baking, decorating, coloring, painting, music, creating software or a spreadsheet? The possibilities are endless.

_____
_____
_____

MORNING HABITS

What are the habits I want to build, increase or pay attention to? Sleep, water, meditation and journaling are the ones that are high on my list, what else do you want to add?

- ☐ 1. My time to get up is _____ am.
- ☐ 2. I will drink _____ glasses of water.
- ☐ 3. I did _____ minutes of Meditation.
- ☐ 4. I Journaled this morning.
- ☐ 5. _____
- ☐ 6. _____

Today's Affirmations

Today's affirmations? I am creative, I am pursuing my dreams today, I am open to possibilities. What positive, present, personal statement are you making for yourself today? Repeat it at least 3 times today.

_____
_____
_____

One action I will take today to make myself or my life better.
Today I will try a new food, today I will go to the gym, today I will send that application, the possibilities are endless. What will you do today to make you life better?

_____
_____

One thing I will do today that is slightly out of my comfort zone.
Those scary things that you think you can't do. What is the worst that will happen? Make that phone call, ask for that raise, create that video, do what ever it takes to pull yourself out of your comfort zone, just one small thing each day will make a huge difference.

_____
_____

Doodle of the Day

All our knowledge has its origin in our perceptions. -Leonardo Da Vinci

How does this quote make you feel?

Notes

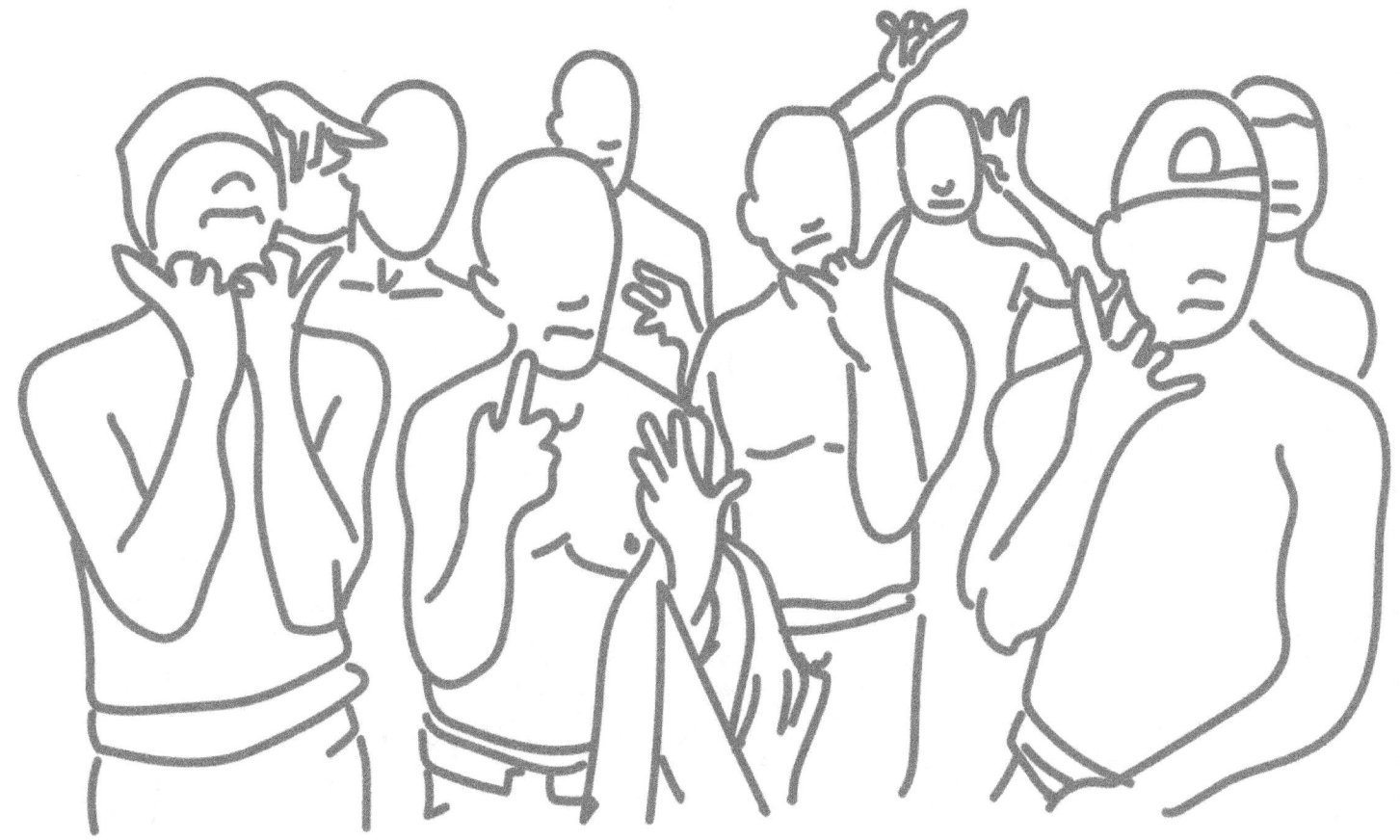

Date _____

> There is no healthier drug than creativity.
> -Nayyirah Waheed

MORNING HABITS

What are the habits I want to build, increase or pay attention to? Sleep, water, meditation and journaling are the ones that are high on my list, what else do you want to add?

- [ ] 1. My time to get up is _____ am.
- [ ] 2. I will drink _____ glasses of water.
- [ ] 3. I did _____ minutes of Meditation.
- [ ] 4. I Journaled this morning.
- [ ] 5. _____
- [ ] 6. _____

Today's Creative Pursuit

What creativity will I pursue today? Baking, decorating, coloring, painting, music, creating software or a spreadsheet? The possibilities are endless.

_____
_____

Today's Affirmations

Today's affirmations? I am creative, I am pursuing my dreams today, I am open to possibilities. What positive, present, personal statement are you making for yourself today? Repeat it at least 3 times today.

_____
_____

One action I will take today to make myself or my life better.

Today I will try a new food, today I will go to the gym, today I will send that application, the possibilities are endless. What will you do today to make you life better?

_____
_____

One thing I will do today that is slightly out of my comfort zone.

Those scary things that you think you can't do. What is the worst that will happen? Make that phone call, ask for that raise, create that video, do what ever it takes to pull yourself out of your comfort zone, just one small thing each day will make a huge difference.

_____

Doodle of the Day

Look for a long time at what pleases you, and longer still at what pains you. -Colette

How does this quote make you feel?

Notes

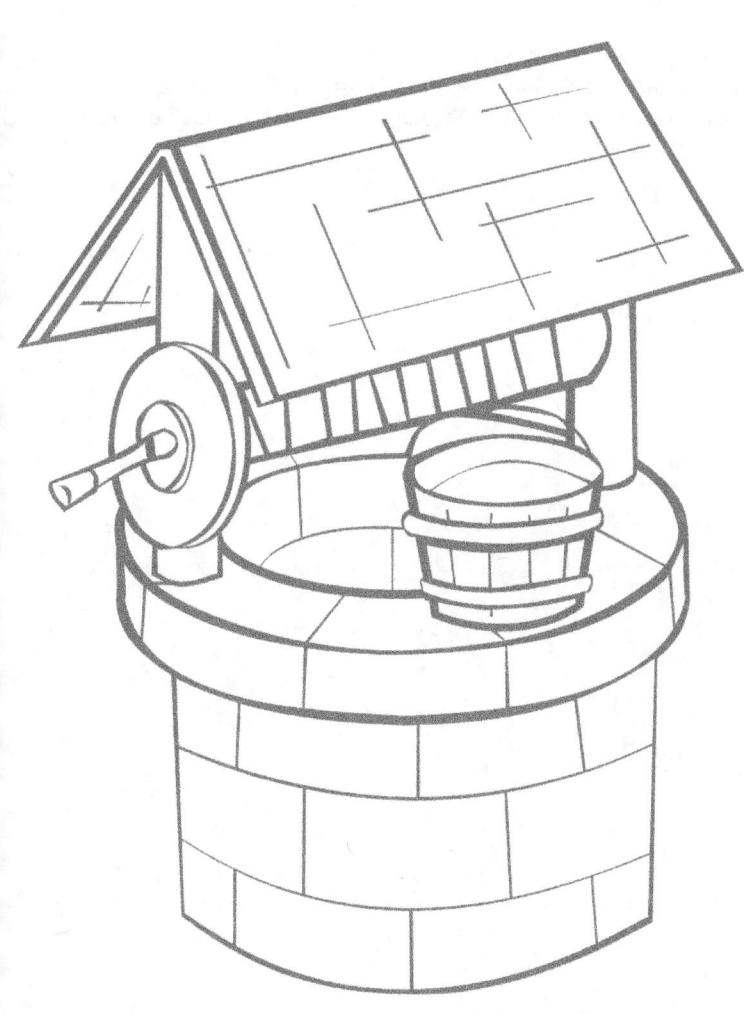

Date _____

> Remember that things are not always as they appear to be... Curiosity creates possibilities and opportunities.
> -Roy T. Bennett

Today's Creative Pursuit

What creativity will I pursue today? Baking, decorating, coloring, painting, music, creating software or a spreadsheet? The possibilities are endless.

_____
_____
_____

MORNING HABITS

What are the habits I want to build, increase or pay attention to? Sleep, water, meditation and journaling are the ones that are high on my list, what else do you want to add?

- ☐ 1. My time to get up is _____ am.
- ☐ 2. I will drink _____ glasses of water.
- ☐ 3. I did _____ minutes of Meditation.
- ☐ 4. I Journaled this morning.
- ☐ 5. _____
- ☐ 6. _____

Today's Affirmations

Today's affirmations? I am creative, I am pursuing my dreams today, I am open to possibilities. What positive, present, personal statement are you making for yourself today? Repeat it at least 3 times today.

_____
_____
_____

One action I will take today to make myself or my life better.
Today I will try a new food, today I will go to the gym, today I will send that application, the possibilities are endless. What will you do today to make you life better?

_____
_____

One thing I will do today that is slightly out of my comfort zone.
Those scary things that you think you can't do. What is the worst that will happen? Make that phone call, ask for that raise, create that video, do what ever it takes to pull yourself out of your comfort zone, just one small thing each day will make a huge difference.

_____
_____

Doodle of the Day

"The desire to create is one of the deepest yearnings of the human soul."
-- Dieter F. Uchtdorf

How does this quote make you feel?

Notes

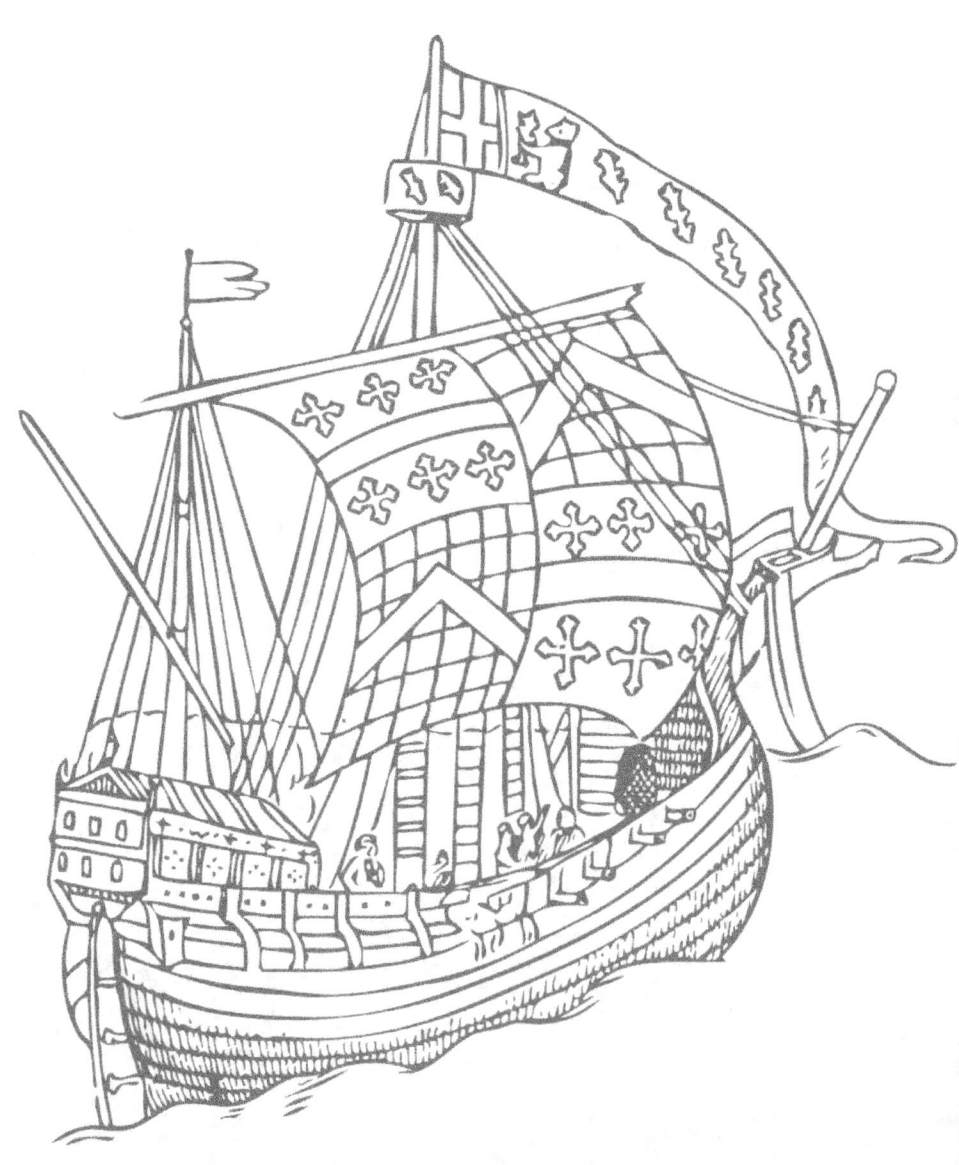

Date _____

> Non-judgment quiets the internal dialogue, and this opens once again the doorway to creativity. -Deepak Chopra

MORNING HABITS

What are the habits I want to build, increase or pay attention to? Sleep, water, meditation and journaling are the ones that are high on my list, what else do you want to add?

- [ ] 1. My time to get up is _____ am.
- [ ] 2. I will drink _____ glasses of water.
- [ ] 3. I did _____ minutes of Meditation.
- [ ] 4. I Journaled this morning.
- [ ] 5. _____
- [ ] 6. _____

Today's Creative Pursuit

What creativity will I pursue today? Baking, decorating, coloring, painting, music, creating software or a spreadsheet? The possibilities are endless.

_____
_____
_____

Today's Affirmations

Today's affirmations? I am creative, I am pursuing my dreams today, I am open to possibilities. What positive, present, personal statement are you making for yourself today? Repeat it at least 3 times today.

_____
_____
_____

One action I will take today to make myself or my life better.

Today I will try a new food, today I will go to the gym, today I will send that application, the possibilities are endless. What will you do today to make you life better?

_____
_____

One thing I will do today that is slightly out of my comfort zone.

Those scary things that you think you can't do. What is the worst that will happen? Make that phone call, ask for that raise, create that video, do what ever it takes to pull yourself out of your comfort zone, just one small thing each day will make a huge difference.

_____
_____

Doodle of the Day

Clear thinking at the wrong moment can stifle creativity. -Karl Lagerfeld

How does this quote make you feel?

Notes

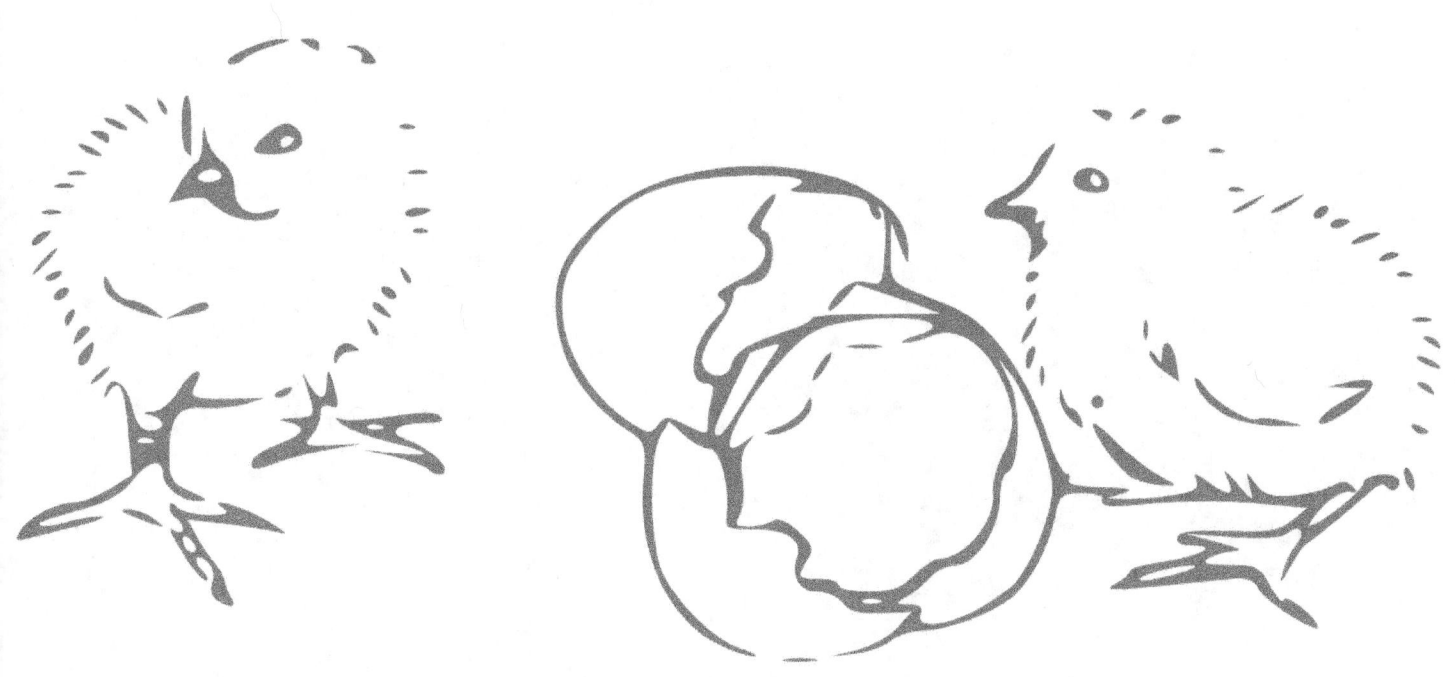

Date _____

> You're mad, bonkers, completely off your head. But I'll tell you a secret. All the best people are. -Lewis Carroll

MORNING HABITS

What are the habits I want to build, increase or pay attention to? Sleep, water, meditation and journaling are the ones that are high on my list, what else do you want to add?

- [ ] 1. My time to get up is _____ am.
- [ ] 2. I will drink _____ glasses of water.
- [ ] 3. I did _____ minutes of Meditation.
- [ ] 4. I Journaled this morning.
- [ ] 5. _____
- [ ] 6. _____

Today's Creative Pursuit

What creativity will I pursue today? Baking, decorating, coloring, painting, music, creating software or a spreadsheet? The possibilities are endless.

_____
_____
_____

Today's Affirmations

Today's affirmations? I am creative, I am pursuing my dreams today, I am open to possibilities. What positive, present, personal statement are you making for yourself today? Repeat it at least 3 times today.

_____
_____
_____

One action I will take today to make myself or my life better.
Today I will try a new food, today I will go to the gym, today I will send that application, the possibilities are endless. What will you do today to make you life better?

_____
_____

One thing I will do today that is slightly out of my comfort zone.
Those scary things that you think you can't do. What is the worst that will happen? Make that phone call, ask for that raise, create that video, do what ever it takes to pull yourself out of your comfort zone, just one small thing each day will make a huge difference.

_____
_____

Doodle of the Day

The principal mark of genius is not perfection but originality, the opening of new frontiers. -Arthur Koestler

How does this quote make you feel?

Notes

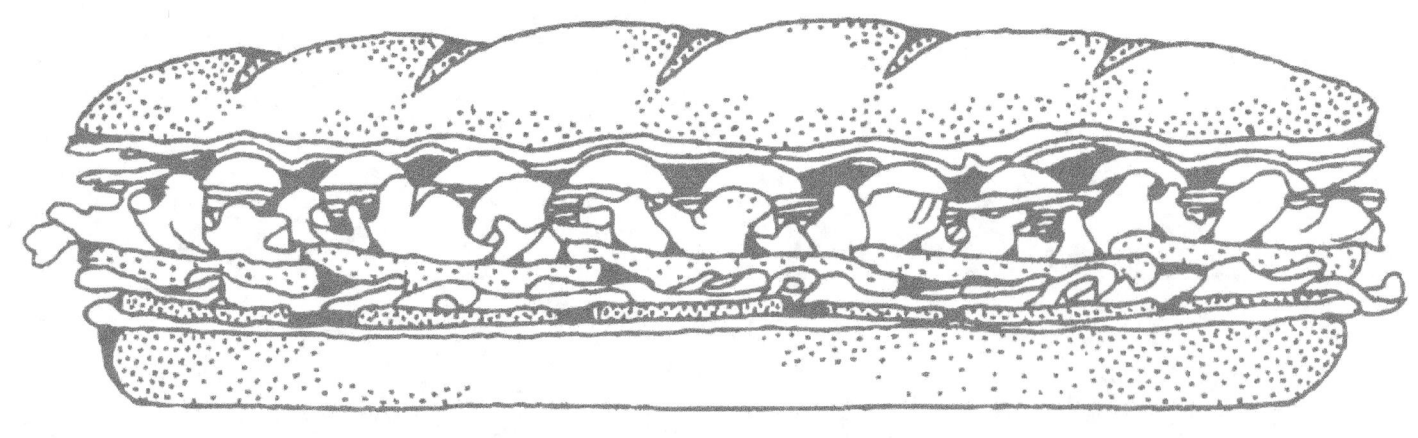

Date _____

> I can always be distracted by love, but eventually I get horny for my creativity.
> -Gilda Radner

MORNING HABITS

What are the habits I want to build, increase or pay attention to? Sleep, water, meditation and journaling are the ones that are high on my list, what else do you want to add?

- ☐ 1. My time to get up is _____ am.
- ☐ 2. I will drink _____ glasses of water.
- ☐ 3. I did _____ minutes of Meditation.
- ☐ 4. I Journaled this morning.
- ☐ 5. _____
- ☐ 6. _____

Today's Creative Pursuit

What creativity will I pursue today? Baking, decorating, coloring, painting, music, creating software or a spreadsheet? The possibilities are endless.

_____
_____
_____

Today's Affirmations

Today's affirmations? I am creative, I am pursuing my dreams today, I am open to possibilities. What positive, present, personal statement are you making for yourself today? Repeat it at least 3 times today.

_____
_____
_____

One action I will take today to make myself or my life better.

Today I will try a new food, today I will go to the gym, today I will send that application, the possibilities are endless. What will you do today to make you life better?

_____
_____

One thing I will do today that is slightly out of my comfort zone.

Those scary things that you think you can't do. What is the worst that will happen? Make that phone call, ask for that raise, create that video, do what ever it takes to pull yourself out of your comfort zone, just one small thing each day will make a huge difference.

_____
_____

Doodle of the Day

Read deeply. Stay open. Continue to wonder.   -Austin Kleon

How does this quote make you feel?

Notes

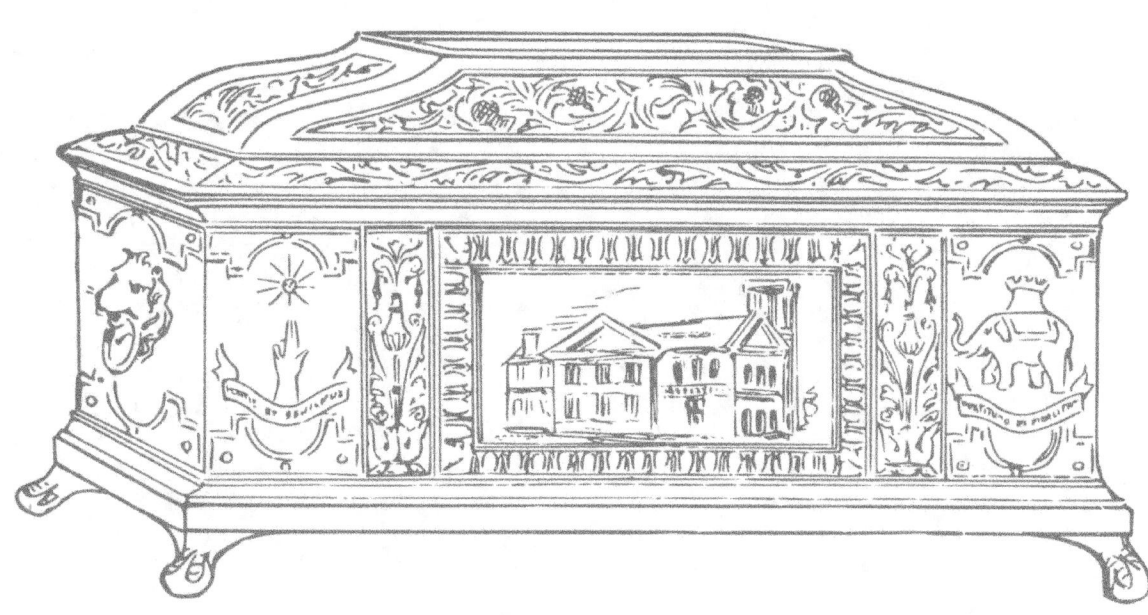

Date _____

I am an artist you know ... it is my right to be odd. -E.A. Bucchianeri

MORNING HABITS

What are the habits I want to build, increase or pay attention to? Sleep, water, meditation and journaling are the ones that are high on my list, what else do you want to add?

- [ ] 1. My time to get up is _____ am.
- [ ] 2. I will drink _____ glasses of water.
- [ ] 3. I did _____ minutes of Meditation.
- [ ] 4. I Journaled this morning.
- [ ] 5. _____
- [ ] 6. _____

Today's Creative Pursuit

What creativity will I pursue today? Baking, decorating, coloring, painting, music, creating software or a spreadsheet? The possibilities are endless.

_____
_____
_____

Today's Affirmations

Today's affirmations? I am creative, I am pursuing my dreams today, I am open to possibilities. What positive, present, personal statement are you making for yourself today? Repeat it at least 3 times today.

_____
_____

One action I will take today to make myself or my life better.

Today I will try a new food, today I will go to the gym, today I will send that application, the possibilities are endless. What will you do today to make you life better?

_____
_____

One thing I will do today that is slightly out of my comfort zone.

Those scary things that you think you can't do. What is the worst that will happen? Make that phone call, ask for that raise, create that video, do what ever it takes to pull yourself out of your comfort zone, just one small thing each day will make a huge difference.

_____
_____

Doodle of the Day

You don't make art out of good intentions. -Gustave Flaubert

How does this quote make you feel?

Notes

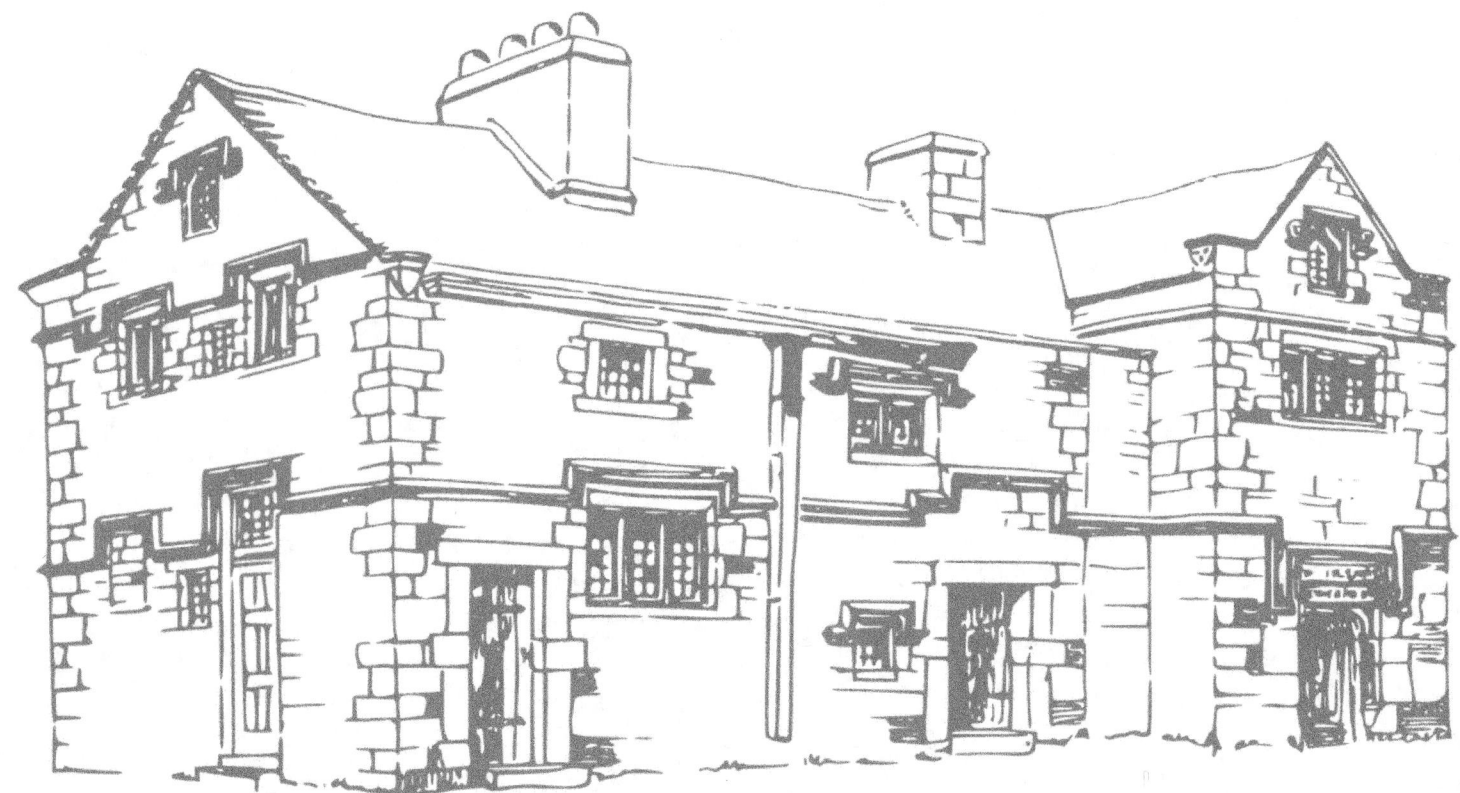

Date _____

> Human salvation lies in the hands of the creatively maladjusted.
> -Martin Luther King Jr.

MORNING HABITS

What are the habits I want to build, increase or pay attention to? Sleep, water, meditation and journaling are the ones that are high on my list, what else do you want to add?

- [ ] 1. My time to get up is _____ am.
- [ ] 2. I will drink _____ glasses of water.
- [ ] 3. I did _____ minutes of Meditation.
- [ ] 4. I Journaled this morning.
- [ ] 5. _____
- [ ] 6. _____

Today's Creative Pursuit

What creativity will I pursue today? Baking, decorating, coloring, painting, music, creating software or a spreadsheet? The possibilities are endless.

_____
_____
_____

Today's Affirmations

Today's affirmations? I am creative, I am pursuing my dreams today, I am open to possibilities. What positive, present, personal statement are you making for yourself today? Repeat it at least 3 times today.

_____
_____
_____

One action I will take today to make myself or my life better.

Today I will try a new food, today I will go to the gym, today I will send that application, the possibilities are endless. What will you do today to make you life better?

_____
_____

One thing I will do today that is slightly out of my comfort zone.

Those scary things that you think you can't do. What is the worst that will happen? Make that phone call, ask for that raise, create that video, do what ever it takes to pull yourself out of your comfort zone, just one small thing each day will make a huge difference.

_____

Doodle of the Day

Creative activity is a type of learning process where the teacher and pupil are located in the same individual. -Arthur Koestler

How does this quote make you feel?

Notes

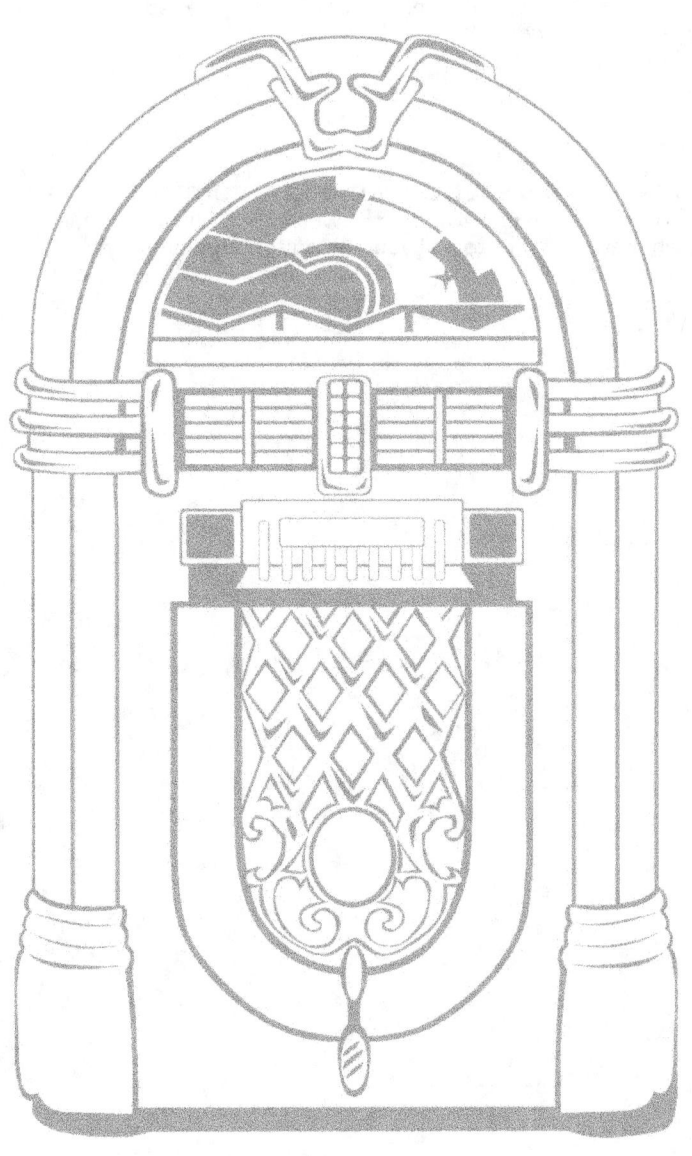

Date _____

> People like you must create. If you don't create, you will become a menace to society. -Maria Semple

MORNING HABITS

What are the habits I want to build, increase or pay attention to? Sleep, water, meditation and journaling are the ones that are high on my list, what else do you want to add?

- [ ] 1. My time to get up is _____ am.
- [ ] 2. I will drink _____ glasses of water.
- [ ] 3. I did _____ minutes of Meditation.
- [ ] 4. I Journaled this morning.
- [ ] 5. _____
- [ ] 6. _____

Today's Creative Pursuit

What creativity will I pursue today? Baking, decorating, coloring, painting, music, creating software or a spreadsheet? The possibilities are endless.

_____
_____
_____

Today's Affirmations

Today's affirmations? I am creative, I am pursuing my dreams today, I am open to possibilities. What positive, present, personal statement are you making for yourself today? Repeat it at least 3 times today.

_____
_____
_____

One action I will take today to make myself or my life better.

Today I will try a new food, today I will go to the gym, today I will send that application, the possibilities are endless. What will you do today to make you life better?

_____
_____

One thing I will do today that is slightly out of my comfort zone.

Those scary things that you think you can't do. What is the worst that will happen? Make that phone call, ask for that raise, create that video, do what ever it takes to pull yourself out of your comfort zone, just one small thing each day will make a huge difference.

_____

Doodle of the Day

Creative power is mightier than its possessor. -C.G. Jung

How does this quote make you feel?

Notes

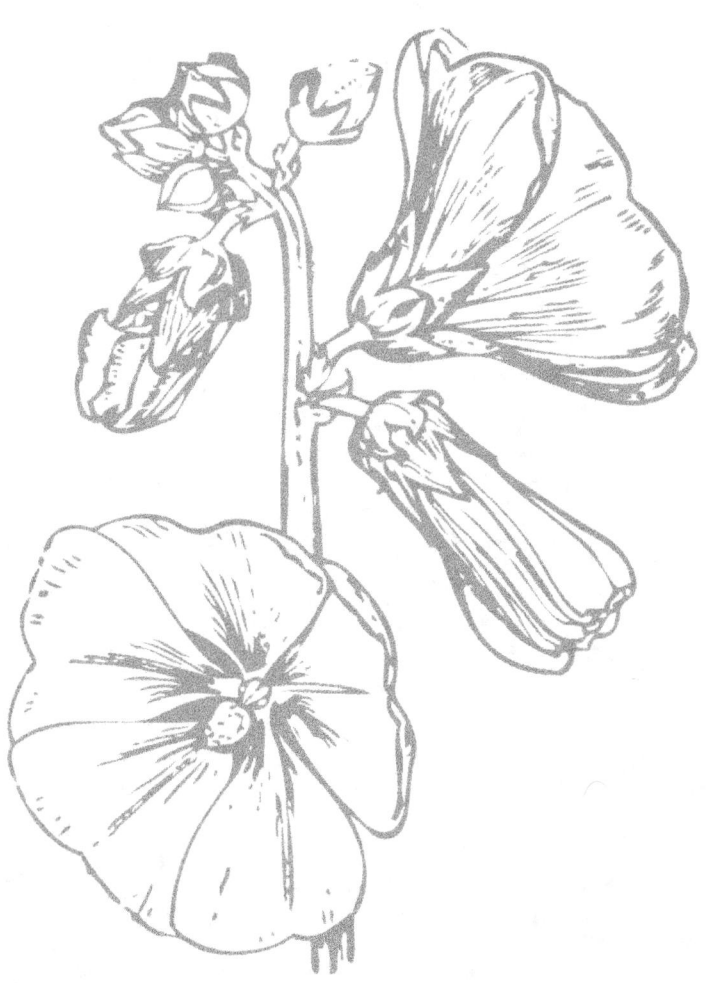

Date _____

> Creativity comes from trust. Trust your instincts. And never hope more than you work. -Rita Mae Brown

MORNING HABITS

What are the habits I want to build, increase or pay attention to? Sleep, water, meditation and journaling are the ones that are high on my list, what else do you want to add?

- [ ] 1. My time to get up is _____ am.
- [ ] 2. I will drink _____ glasses of water.
- [ ] 3. I did _____ minutes of Meditation.
- [ ] 4. I Journaled this morning.
- [ ] 5. _____
- [ ] 6. _____

Today's Creative Pursuit

What creativity will I pursue today? Baking, decorating, coloring, painting, music, creating software or a spreadsheet? The possibilities are endless.

_____
_____
_____

Today's Affirmations

Today's affirmations? I am creative, I am pursuing my dreams today, I am open to possibilities. What positive, present, personal statement are you making for yourself today? Repeat it at least 3 times today.

_____
_____
_____

One action I will take today to make myself or my life better.

Today I will try a new food, today I will go to the gym, today I will send that application, the possibilities are endless. What will you do today to make you life better?

_____
_____

One thing I will do today that is slightly out of my comfort zone.

Those scary things that you think you can't do. What is the worst that will happen? Make that phone call, ask for that raise, create that video, do what ever it takes to pull yourself out of your comfort zone, just one small thing each day will make a huge difference.

_____
_____

Doodle of the Day

To create art with all the passion in one's soul is to live art with all the beauty in one's heart. -Aberjhani

How does this quote make you feel?

Notes

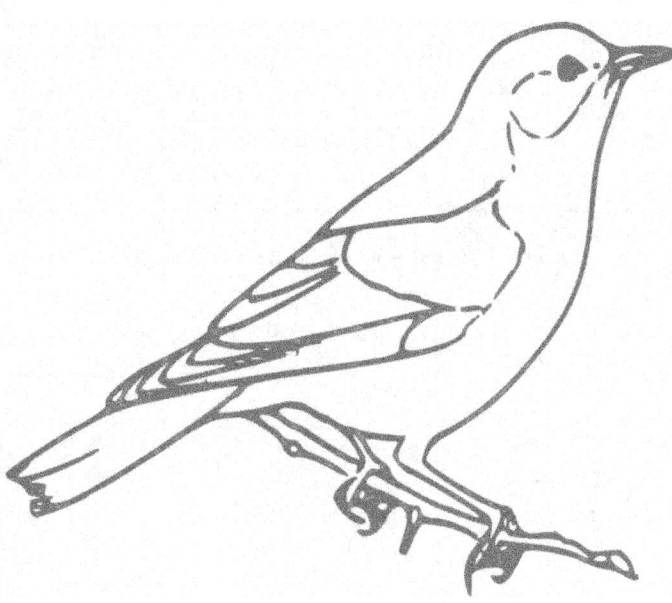

Date _____

> Creativity is a continual surprise.
> -Ray Bradbury

MORNING HABITS

What are the habits I want to build, increase or pay attention to? Sleep, water, meditation and journaling are the ones that are high on my list, what else do you want to add?

- [ ] 1. My time to get up is _____ am.
- [ ] 2. I will drink _____ glasses of water.
- [ ] 3. I did _____ minutes of Meditation.
- [ ] 4. I Journaled this morning.
- [ ] 5. _____
- [ ] 6. _____

Today's Creative Pursuit

What creativity will I pursue today? Baking, decorating, coloring, painting, music, creating software or a spreadsheet? The possibilities are endless.

_____
_____
_____

Today's Affirmations

Today's affirmations? I am creative, I am pursuing my dreams today, I am open to possibilities. What positive, present, personal statement are you making for yourself today? Repeat it at least 3 times today.

_____
_____
_____

One action I will take today to make myself or my life better.

Today I will try a new food, today I will go to the gym, today I will send that application, the possibilities are endless. What will you do today to make you life better?

_____
_____

One thing I will do today that is slightly out of my comfort zone.

Those scary things that you think you can't do. What is the worst that will happen? Make that phone call, ask for that raise, create that video, do what ever it takes to pull yourself out of your comfort zone, just one small thing each day will make a huge difference.

_____
_____

Doodle of the Day

Creativity arises from our ability to see things from many different angles.
-Keri Smith

How does this quote make you feel?

Notes

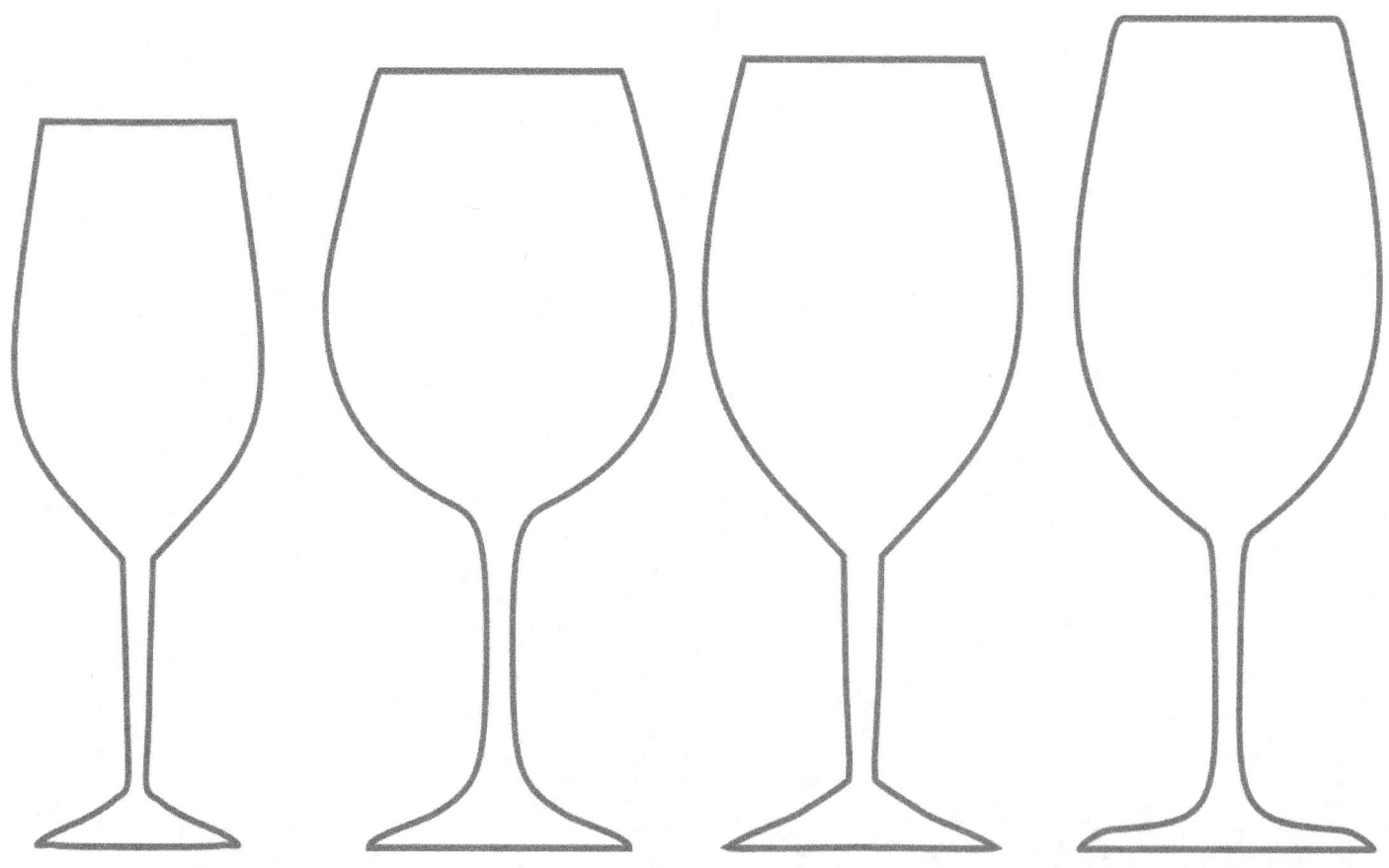

Date _____

> The truth is that creative activity is one that involves the entire self - our emotions, our levels of energy, our characters, and our minds.
> -Robert Greene

MORNING HABITS

What are the habits I want to build, increase or pay attention to? Sleep, water, meditation and journaling are the ones that are high on my list, what else do you want to add?

- [ ] 1. My time to get up is _____ am.
- [ ] 2. I will drink _____ glasses of water.
- [ ] 3. I did _____ minutes of Meditation.
- [ ] 4. I Journaled this morning.
- [ ] 5. _____
- [ ] 6. _____

Today's Creative Pursuit

What creativity will I pursue today? Baking, decorating, coloring, painting, music, creating software or a spreadsheet? The possibilities are endless.

_____
_____
_____

Today's Affirmations

Today's affirmations? I am creative, I am pursuing my dreams today, I am open to possibilities. What positive, present, personal statement are you making for yourself today? Repeat it at least 3 times today.

_____
_____
_____

One action I will take today to make myself or my life better.

Today I will try a new food, today I will go to the gym, today I will send that application, the possibilities are endless. What will you do today to make you life better?

_____
_____

One thing I will do today that is slightly out of my comfort zone.

Those scary things that you think you can't do. What is the worst that will happen? Make that phone call, ask for that raise, create that video, do what ever it takes to pull yourself out of your comfort zone, just one small thing each day will make a huge difference.

_____
_____

Doodle of the Day

We nurture our creativity when we release our inner child. Let it run and roam free. It will take you on a brighter journey. -Serina Hartwell

How does this quote make you feel?

Notes

Date _____

> The unlike is joined together, and from differences results the most beautiful harmony. -Heraclitus

MORNING HABITS

What are the habits I want to build, increase or pay attention to? Sleep, water, meditation and journaling are the ones that are high on my list, what else do you want to add?

1. My time to get up is _____ am.
2. I will drink _____ glasses of water.
3. I did _____ minutes of Meditation.
4. I Journaled this morning.
5. _____
6. _____

Today's Creative Pursuit

What creativity will I pursue today? Baking, decorating, coloring, painting, music, creating software or a spreadsheet? The possibilities are endless.

_____
_____
_____

Today's Affirmations

Today's affirmations? I am creative, I am pursuing my dreams today, I am open to possibilities. What positive, present, personal statement are you making for yourself today? Repeat it at least 3 times today.

_____
_____
_____

One action I will take today to make myself or my life better.

Today I will try a new food, today I will go to the gym, today I will send that application, the possibilities are endless. What will you do today to make you life better?

_____
_____

One thing I will do today that is slightly out of my comfort zone.

Those scary things that you think you can't do. What is the worst that will happen? Make that phone call, ask for that raise, create that video, do what ever it takes to pull yourself out of your comfort zone, just one small thing each day will make a huge difference.

_____
_____

Doodle of the Day

Create. Not for the money. Not for the fame. Not for the recognition. But for the pure joy of creating something. -Ernest Barbaric

How does this quote make you feel?

Notes

Date _____

> My future starts when I wake up every morning. Every day I find something creative to do with my life. -Miles Davis

MORNING HABITS

What are the habits I want to build, increase or pay attention to? Sleep, water, meditation and journaling are the ones that are high on my list, what else do you want to add?

- [ ] 1. My time to get up is _____ am.
- [ ] 2. I will drink _____ glasses of water.
- [ ] 3. I did _____ minutes of Meditation.
- [ ] 4. I Journaled this morning.
- [ ] 5. _____
- [ ] 6. _____

Today's Creative Pursuit

What creativity will I pursue today? Baking, decorating, coloring, painting, music, creating software or a spreadsheet? The possibilities are endless.

_____
_____
_____

Today's Affirmations

Today's affirmations? I am creative, I am pursuing my dreams today, I am open to possibilities. What positive, present, personal statement are you making for yourself today? Repeat it at least 3 times today.

_____
_____
_____

One action I will take today to make myself or my life better.

Today I will try a new food, today I will go to the gym, today I will send that application, the possibilities are endless. What will you do today to make you life better?

_____
_____

One thing I will do today that is slightly out of my comfort zone.

Those scary things that you think you can't do. What is the worst that will happen? Make that phone call, ask for that raise, create that video, do what ever it takes to pull yourself out of your comfort zone, just one small thing each day will make a huge difference.

_____
_____

Doodle of the Day

We need our Arts to teach us how to breathe. -Ray Bradbury

How does this quote make you feel?

Notes

Date _____

> You can't keep bitch-slapping your creativity, or it'll run away and find a new pimp. -George Meyer

Today's Creative Pursuit

What creativity will I pursue today? Baking, decorating, coloring, painting, music, creating software or a spreadsheet? The possibilities are endless.

_____
_____
_____

MORNING HABITS

What are the habits I want to build, increase or pay attention to? Sleep, water, meditation and journaling are the ones that are high on my list, what else do you want to add?

☐ 1. My time to get up is _____ am.
☐ 2. I will drink _____ glasses of water.
☐ 3. I did _____ minutes of Meditation.
☐ 4. I Journaled this morning.
☐ 5. _____
☐ 6. _____

Today's Affirmations

Today's affirmations? I am creative, I am pursuing my dreams today, I am open to possibilities. What positive, present, personal statement are you making for yourself today? Repeat it at least 3 times today.

_____
_____
_____

One action I will take today to make myself or my life better.

Today I will try a new food, today I will go to the gym, today I will send that application, the possibilities are endless. What will you do today to make you life better?

_____
_____

One thing I will do today that is slightly out of my comfort zone.

Those scary things that you think you can't do. What is the worst that will happen? Make that phone call, ask for that raise, create that video, do what ever it takes to pull yourself out of your comfort zone, just one small thing each day will make a huge difference.

_____
_____

Doodle of the Day

It's an artist's right to rebel against the world's stupidity. -E.A. Bucchianeri

How does this quote make you feel?

Notes

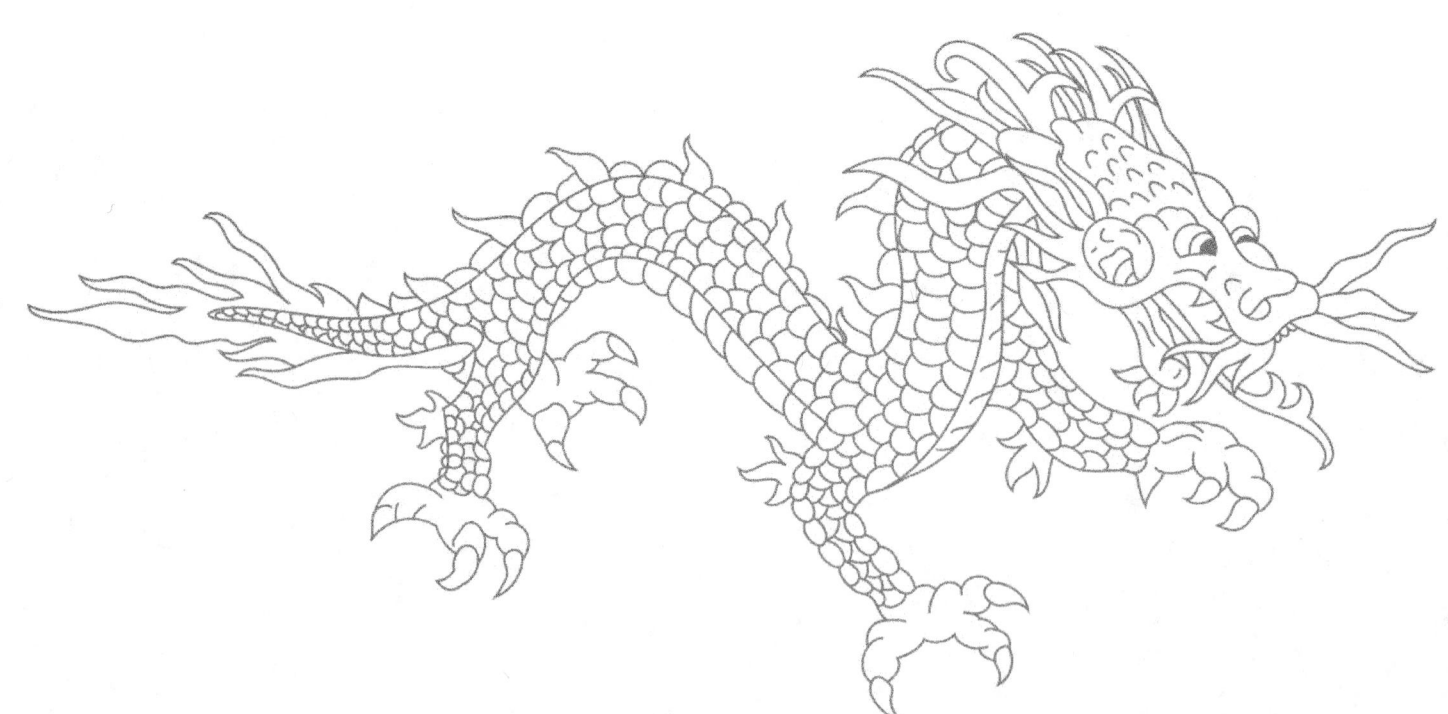

Date _____

> Where we fall are the stepping-stones for our journey. -Lolly Daskal

MORNING HABITS

What are the habits I want to build, increase or pay attention to? Sleep, water, meditation and journaling are the ones that are high on my list, what else do you want to add?

- [ ] 1. My time to get up is _____ am.
- [ ] 2. I will drink _____ glasses of water.
- [ ] 3. I did _____ minutes of Meditation.
- [ ] 4. I Journaled this morning.
- [ ] 5. _____
- [ ] 6. _____

Today's Creative Pursuit

What creativity will I pursue today? Baking, decorating, coloring, painting, music, creating software or a spreadsheet? The possibilities are endless.

_____
_____
_____

Today's Affirmations

Today's affirmations? I am creative, I am pursuing my dreams today, I am open to possibilities. What positive, present, personal statement are you making for yourself today? Repeat it at least 3 times today.

_____
_____
_____

One action I will take today to make myself or my life better.

Today I will try a new food, today I will go to the gym, today I will send that application, the possibilities are endless. What will you do today to make you life better?

_____
_____

One thing I will do today that is slightly out of my comfort zone.

Those scary things that you think you can't do. What is the worst that will happen? Make that phone call, ask for that raise, create that video, do what ever it takes to pull yourself out of your comfort zone, just one small thing each day will make a huge difference.

_____
_____

Doodle of the Day

Life in itself has no meaning. Life is an opportunity to create meaning. -Osho

How does this quote make you feel?

Notes

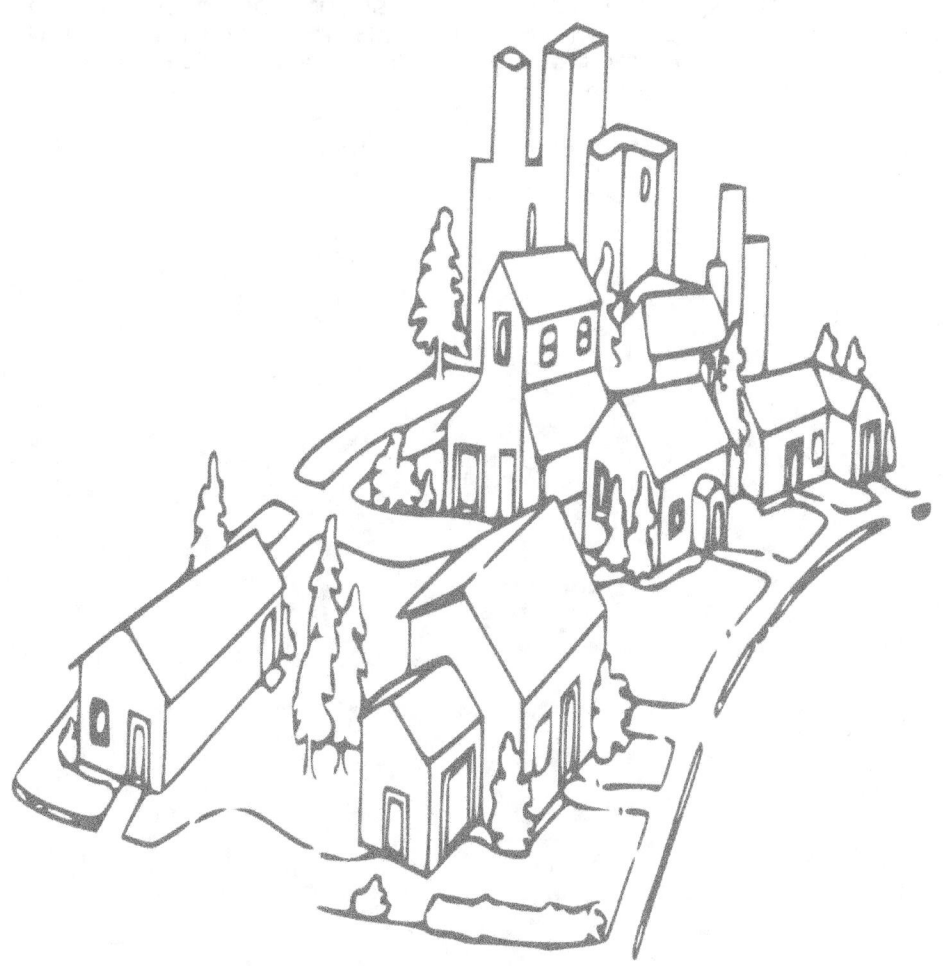

Date _____

> Imperfection inspires invention, imagination, creativity. It stimulates. The more I feel imperfect, the more I feel alive.
> -Jhumpa Lahiri

MORNING HABITS

What are the habits I want to build, increase or pay attention to? Sleep, water, meditation and journaling are the ones that are high on my list, what else do you want to add?

1. My time to get up is _____ am.
2. I will drink _____ glasses of water.
3. I did _____ minutes of Meditation.
4. I Journaled this morning.
5. _____
6. _____

Today's Creative Pursuit

What creativity will I pursue today? Baking, decorating, coloring, painting, music, creating software or a spreadsheet? The possibilities are endless.

_____
_____
_____

Today's Affirmations

Today's affirmations? I am creative, I am pursuing my dreams today, I am open to possibilities. What positive, present, personal statement are you making for yourself today? Repeat it at least 3 times today.

_____
_____
_____

One action I will take today to make myself or my life better.

Today I will try a new food, today I will go to the gym, today I will send that application, the possibilities are endless. What will you do today to make you life better?

_____
_____

One thing I will do today that is slightly out of my comfort zone.

Those scary things that you think you can't do. What is the worst that will happen? Make that phone call, ask for that raise, create that video, do what ever it takes to pull yourself out of your comfort zone, just one small thing each day will make a huge difference.

_____
_____

Doodle of the Day

Creativity can solve almost any problem. The creative act, the defeat of habit by originality, overcomes everything. -George Lois

How does this quote make you feel?

Notes

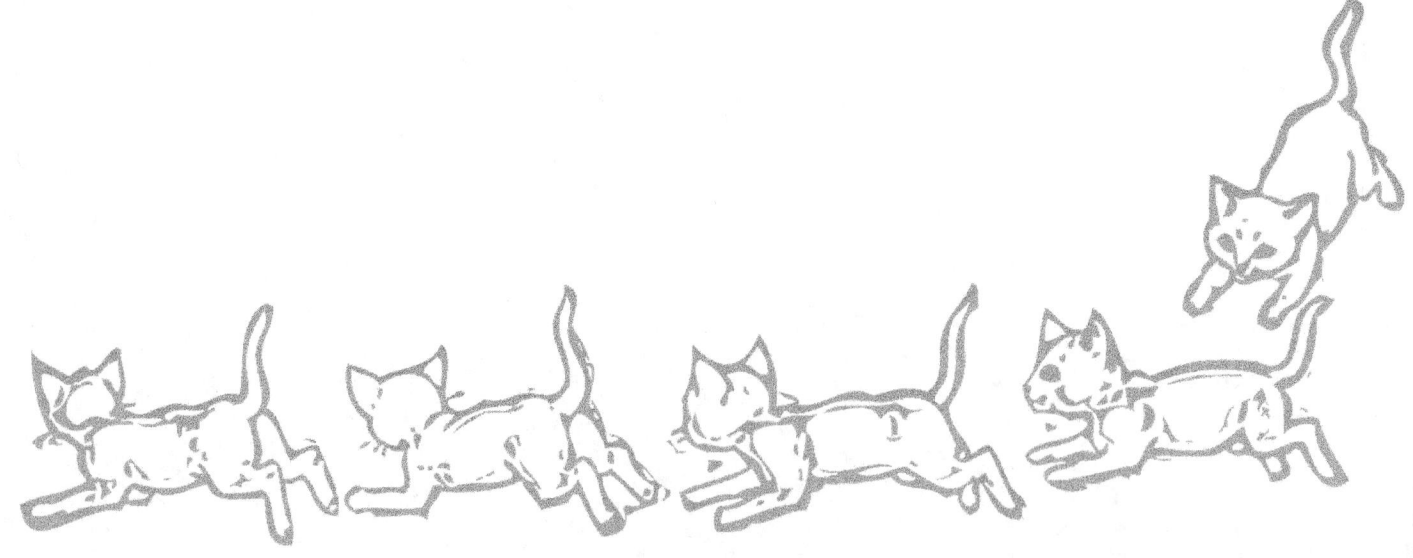

Date _____

> What if the very reason you were created was to be creative?
> -Michelle Dennis Evans

MORNING HABITS

What are the habits I want to build, increase or pay attention to? Sleep, water, meditation and journaling are the ones that are high on my list, what else do you want to add?

☐ 1. My time to get up is _____ am.
☐ 2. I will drink _____ glasses of water.
☐ 3. I did _____ minutes of Meditation.
☐ 4. I Journaled this morning.
☐ 5. _____
☐ 6. _____

Today's Creative Pursuit

What creativity will I pursue today? Baking, decorating, coloring, painting, music, creating software or a spreadsheet? The possibilities are endless.

_____
_____
_____

Today's Affirmations

Today's affirmations? I am creative, I am pursuing my dreams today, I am open to possibilities. What positive, present, personal statement are you making for yourself today? Repeat it at least 3 times today.

_____
_____
_____

One action I will take today to make myself or my life better.
Today I will try a new food, today I will go to the gym, today I will send that application, the possibilities are endless. What will you do today to make you life better?

_____
_____

One thing I will do today that is slightly out of my comfort zone.
Those scary things that you think you can't do. What is the worst that will happen? Make that phone call, ask for that raise, create that video, do what ever it takes to pull yourself out of your comfort zone, just one small thing each day will make a huge difference.

_____
_____

Doodle of the Day

Sometimes an artist's first invention is herself. -Stephanie Vaughn

How does this quote make you feel?

Notes

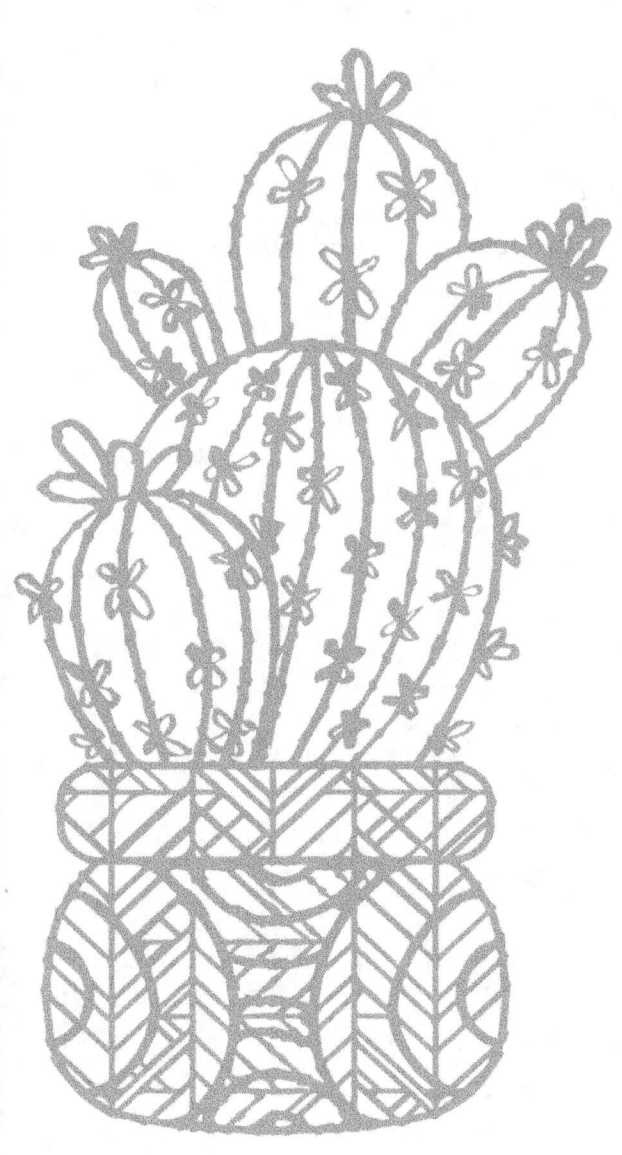

Date _____

> They're only crayons. You didn't fear them in Kindergarten, why fear them now?
> -Hugh MacLeod

MORNING HABITS

What are the habits I want to build, increase or pay attention to? Sleep, water, meditation and journaling are the ones that are high on my list, what else do you want to add?

1. My time to get up is _____ am.
2. I will drink _____ glasses of water.
3. I did _____ minutes of Meditation.
4. I Journaled this morning.
5. _____
6. _____

Today's Creative Pursuit

What creativity will I pursue today? Baking, decorating, coloring, painting, music, creating software or a spreadsheet? The possibilities are endless.

_____
_____
_____

Today's Affirmations

Today's affirmations? I am creative, I am pursuing my dreams today, I am open to possibilities. What positive, present, personal statement are you making for yourself today? Repeat it at least 3 times today.

_____
_____
_____

One action I will take today to make myself or my life better.

Today I will try a new food, today I will go to the gym, today I will send that application, the possibilities are endless. What will you do today to make you life better?

_____
_____

One thing I will do today that is slightly out of my comfort zone.

Those scary things that you think you can't do. What is the worst that will happen? Make that phone call, ask for that raise, create that video, do what ever it takes to pull yourself out of your comfort zone, just one small thing each day will make a huge difference.

_____

Doodle of the Day

Find your authentic voice, become vulnerable, and then put yourself out there.
-Meredith Brooks

How does this quote make you feel?

Notes

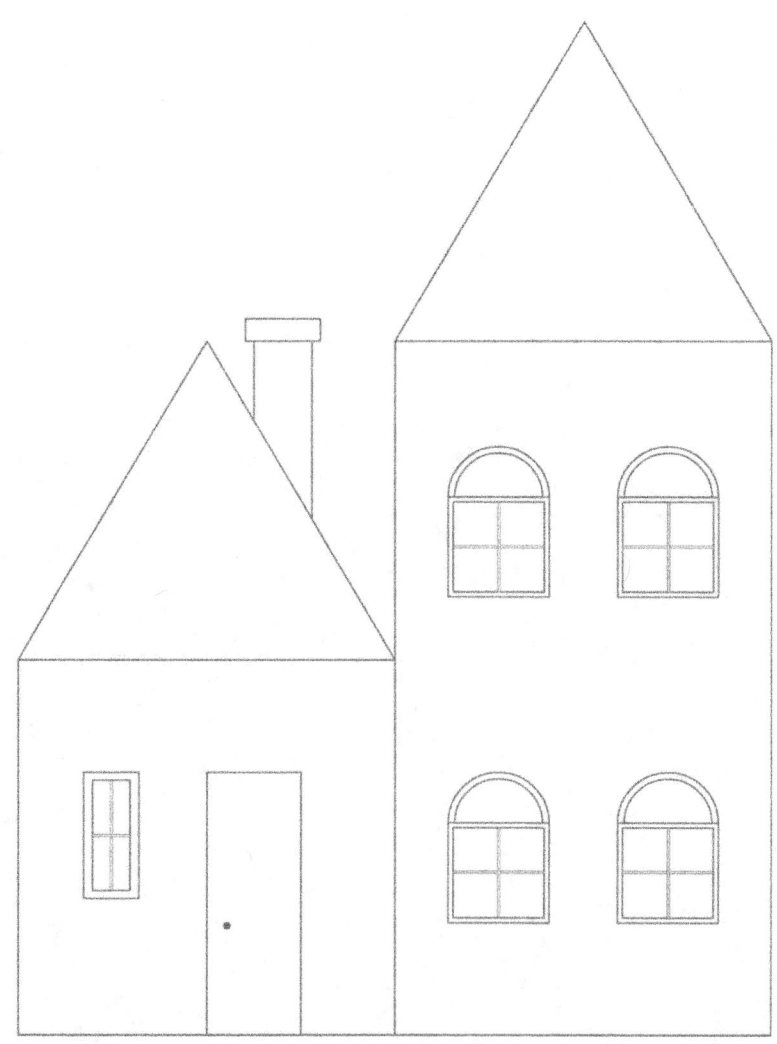

Date _____

> Creativity is the brain's invisible muscle --
> that when used and exercised routinely --
> becomes better and stronger.
> -Ashley Ormon

Today's Creative Pursuit

What creativity will I pursue today? Baking, decorating, coloring, painting, music, creating software or a spreadsheet? The possibilities are endless.

_____
_____
_____

MORNING HABITS

What are the habits I want to build, increase or pay attention to? Sleep, water, meditation and journaling are the ones that are high on my list, what else do you want to add?

- [ ] 1. My time to get up is _____ am.
- [ ] 2. I will drink _____ glasses of water.
- [ ] 3. I did _____ minutes of Meditation.
- [ ] 4. I Journaled this morning.
- [ ] 5. _____
- [ ] 6. _____

Today's Affirmations

Today's affirmations? I am creative, I am pursuing my dreams today, I am open to possibilities. What positive, present, personal statement are you making for yourself today? Repeat it at least 3 times today.

_____
_____
_____

One action I will take today to make myself or my life better.
Today I will try a new food, today I will go to the gym, today I will send that application, the possibilities are endless. What will you do today to make you life better?

_____
_____

One thing I will do today that is slightly out of my comfort zone.
Those scary things that you think you can't do. What is the worst that will happen? Make that phone call, ask for that raise, create that video, do what ever it takes to pull yourself out of your comfort zone, just one small thing each day will make a huge difference.

_____
_____

Doodle of the Day

The human spirit lives on creativity and dies in conformity and routine.
-Vilayat Inayat Khan

How does this quote make you feel?

Notes

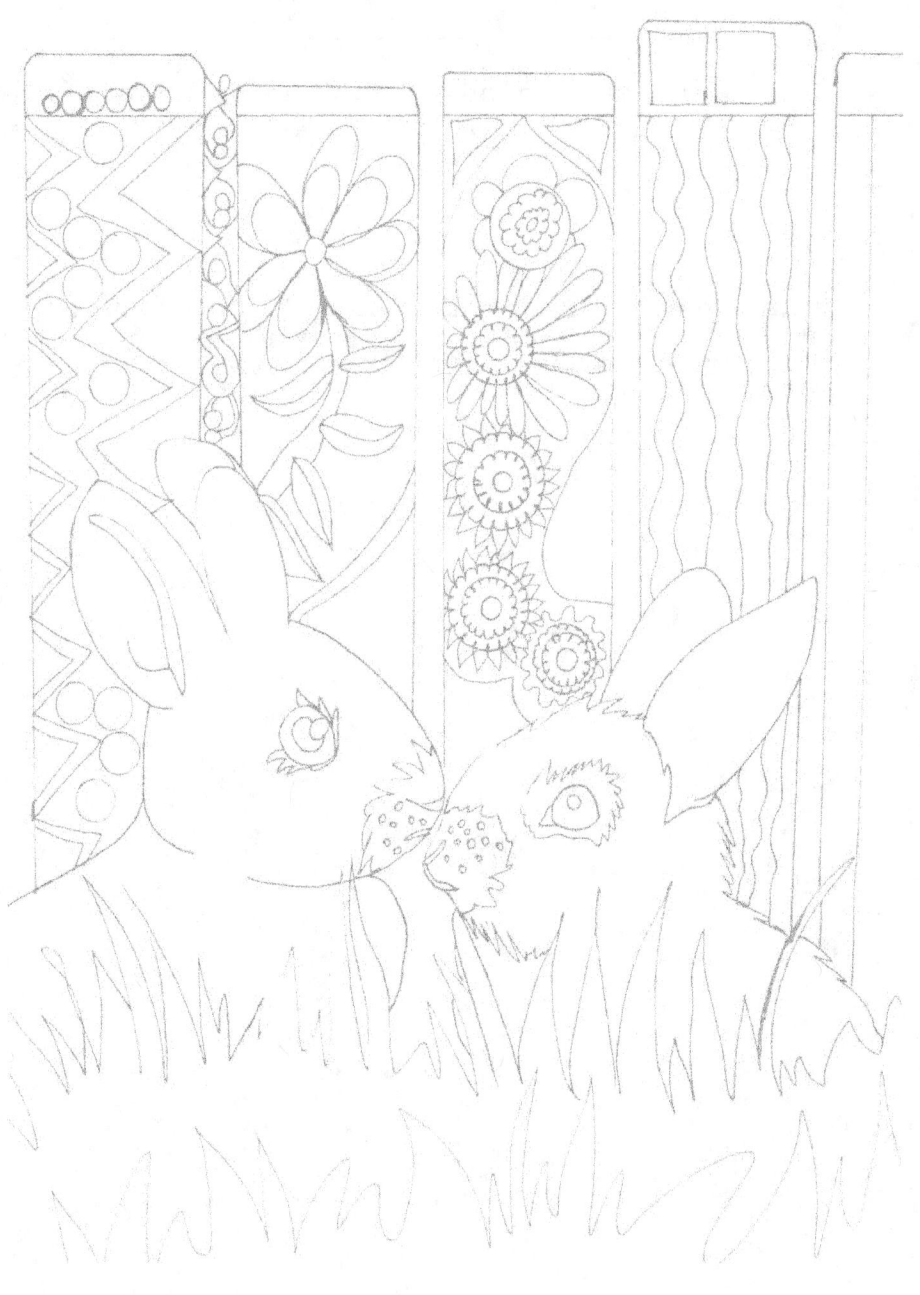

Date _____

> You have to be willing to spend time making things for no known reason.
> -Lynda Barry

MORNING HABITS

What are the habits I want to build, increase or pay attention to? Sleep, water, meditation and journaling are the ones that are high on my list, what else do you want to add?

☐ 1. My time to get up is _____ am.
☐ 2. I will drink _____ glasses of water.
☐ 3. I did _____ minutes of Meditation.
☐ 4. I Journaled this morning.
☐ 5. _____
☐ 6. _____

Today's Creative Pursuit

What creativity will I pursue today? Baking, decorating, coloring, painting, music, creating software or a spreadsheet? The possibilities are endless.

_____
_____
_____

Today's Affirmations

Today's affirmations? I am creative, I am pursuing my dreams today, I am open to possibilities. What positive, present, personal statement are you making for yourself today? Repeat it at least 3 times today.

_____
_____
_____

One action I will take today to make myself or my life better.

Today I will try a new food, today I will go to the gym, today I will send that application, the possibilities are endless. What will you do today to make you life better?

_____
_____

One thing I will do today that is slightly out of my comfort zone.

Those scary things that you think you can't do. What is the worst that will happen? Make that phone call, ask for that raise, create that video, do what ever it takes to pull yourself out of your comfort zone, just one small thing each day will make a huge difference.

_____
_____

Doodle of the Day

We need creativity in order to break free from the temporary structures that have been set up by a particular sequence of experience. -Edward de Bono

How does this quote make you feel?

Notes

Date _____

> For the person with creative potential there is no wholeness except in using it.
> -Robert K. Greenleaf

MORNING HABITS

What are the habits I want to build, increase or pay attention to? Sleep, water, meditation and journaling are the ones that are high on my list, what else do you want to add?

- [ ] 1. My time to get up is _____ am.
- [ ] 2. I will drink _____ glasses of water.
- [ ] 3. I did _____ minutes of Meditation.
- [ ] 4. I Journaled this morning.
- [ ] 5. _____
- [ ] 6. _____

Today's Creative Pursuit

What creativity will I pursue today? Baking, decorating, coloring, painting, music, creating software or a spreadsheet? The possibilities are endless.

_____
_____
_____

Today's Affirmations

Today's affirmations? I am creative, I am pursuing my dreams today, I am open to possibilities. What positive, present, personal statement are you making for yourself today? Repeat it at least 3 times today.

_____
_____
_____

One action I will take today to make myself or my life better.

Today I will try a new food, today I will go to the gym, today I will send that application, the possibilities are endless. What will you do today to make you life better?

_____
_____

One thing I will do today that is slightly out of my comfort zone.

Those scary things that you think you can't do. What is the worst that will happen? Make that phone call, ask for that raise, create that video, do what ever it takes to pull yourself out of your comfort zone, just one small thing each day will make a huge difference.

_____
_____

Doodle of the Day

I would rather be an artist than a leader. Ironically, a leader has to follow the rules. -Criss Jami

How does this quote make you feel?

Notes

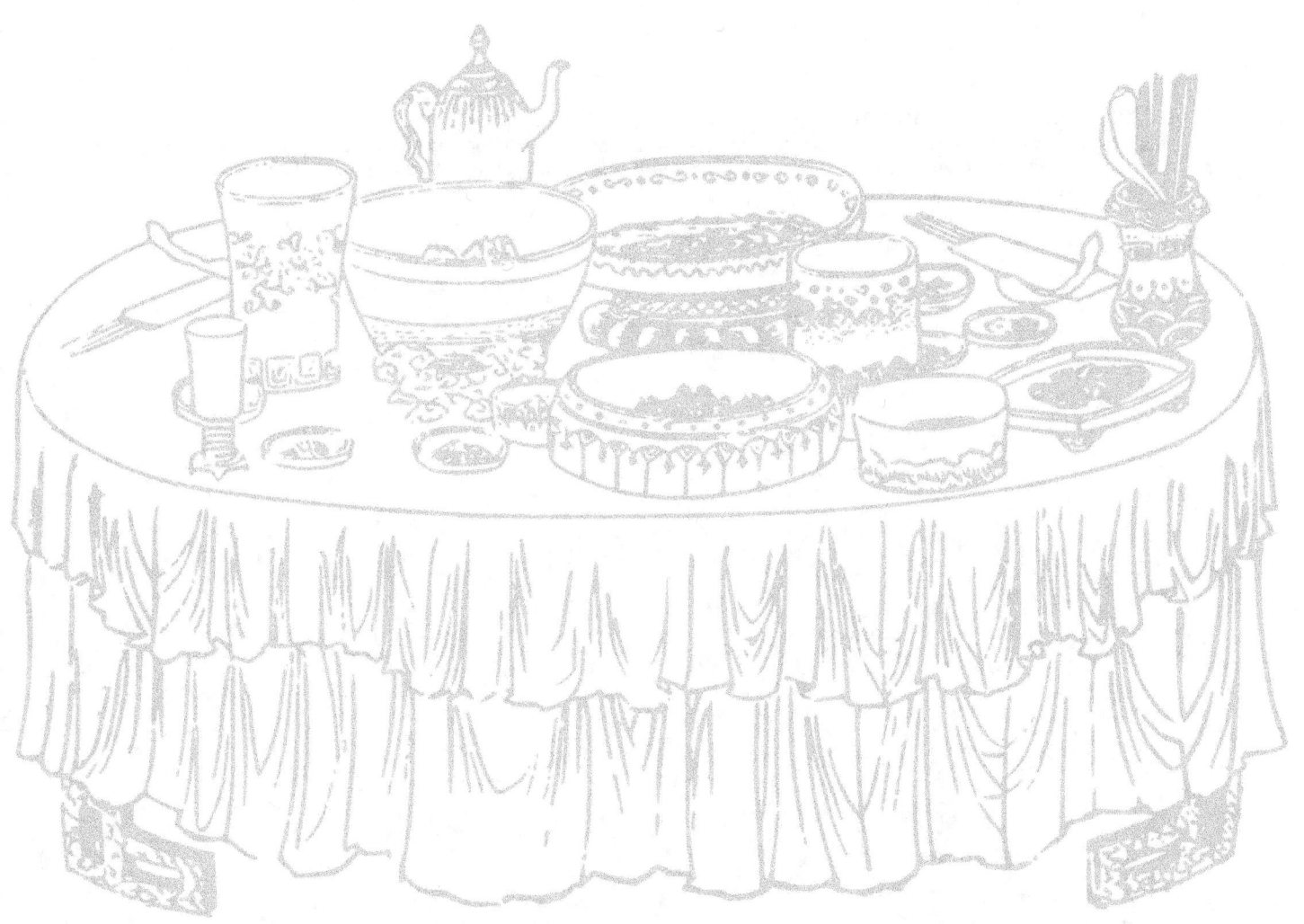

Date _____

> Creativity comes from looking for the unexpected and stepping outside your own experience. -Masaru Ibuka

MORNING HABITS

What are the habits I want to build, increase or pay attention to? Sleep, water, meditation and journaling are the ones that are high on my list, what else do you want to add?

- [ ] 1. My time to get up is _____ am.
- [ ] 2. I will drink _____ glasses of water.
- [ ] 3. I did _____ minutes of Meditation.
- [ ] 4. I Journaled this morning.
- [ ] 5. _____
- [ ] 6. _____

Today's Creative Pursuit

What creativity will I pursue today? Baking, decorating, coloring, painting, music, creating software or a spreadsheet? The possibilities are endless.

_____
_____
_____

Today's Affirmations

Today's affirmations? I am creative, I am pursuing my dreams today, I am open to possibilities. What positive, present, personal statement are you making for yourself today? Repeat it at least 3 times today.

_____
_____
_____

One action I will take today to make myself or my life better.

Today I will try a new food, today I will go to the gym, today I will send that application, the possibilities are endless. What will you do today to make you life better?

_____
_____

One thing I will do today that is slightly out of my comfort zone.

Those scary things that you think you can't do. What is the worst that will happen? Make that phone call, ask for that raise, create that video, do what ever it takes to pull yourself out of your comfort zone, just one small thing each day will make a huge difference.

_____
_____

Doodle of the Day

Rules are a great way to get ideas. All you have to do is break them.
-Jack Foster

How does this quote make you feel?

Notes

Date _____

> Every creative story is different. And every creative story is the same. There was nothing. Now there is something. It's almost like magic. -Jonah Lehrer

Today's Creative Pursuit

What creativity will I pursue today? Baking, decorating, coloring, painting, music, creating software or a spreadsheet? The possibilities are endless.

_____
_____
_____

MORNING HABITS

What are the habits I want to build, increase or pay attention to? Sleep, water, meditation and journaling are the ones that are high on my list, what else do you want to add?

- [ ] 1. My time to get up is _____ am.
- [ ] 2. I will drink _____ glasses of water.
- [ ] 3. I did _____ minutes of Meditation.
- [ ] 4. I Journaled this morning.
- [ ] 5. _____
- [ ] 6. _____

Today's Affirmations

Today's affirmations? I am creative, I am pursuing my dreams today, I am open to possibilities. What positive, present, personal statement are you making for yourself today? Repeat it at least 3 times today.

_____
_____
_____

One action I will take today to make myself or my life better.

Today I will try a new food, today I will go to the gym, today I will send that application, the possibilities are endless. What will you do today to make you life better?

_____
_____

One thing I will do today that is slightly out of my comfort zone.

Those scary things that you think you can't do. What is the worst that will happen? Make that phone call, ask for that raise, create that video, do what ever it takes to pull yourself out of your comfort zone, just one small thing each day will make a huge difference.

_____
_____

Doodle of the Day

Creativity is one of the highest transmissions of love. -Suzy Kassem

How does this quote make you feel?

Notes

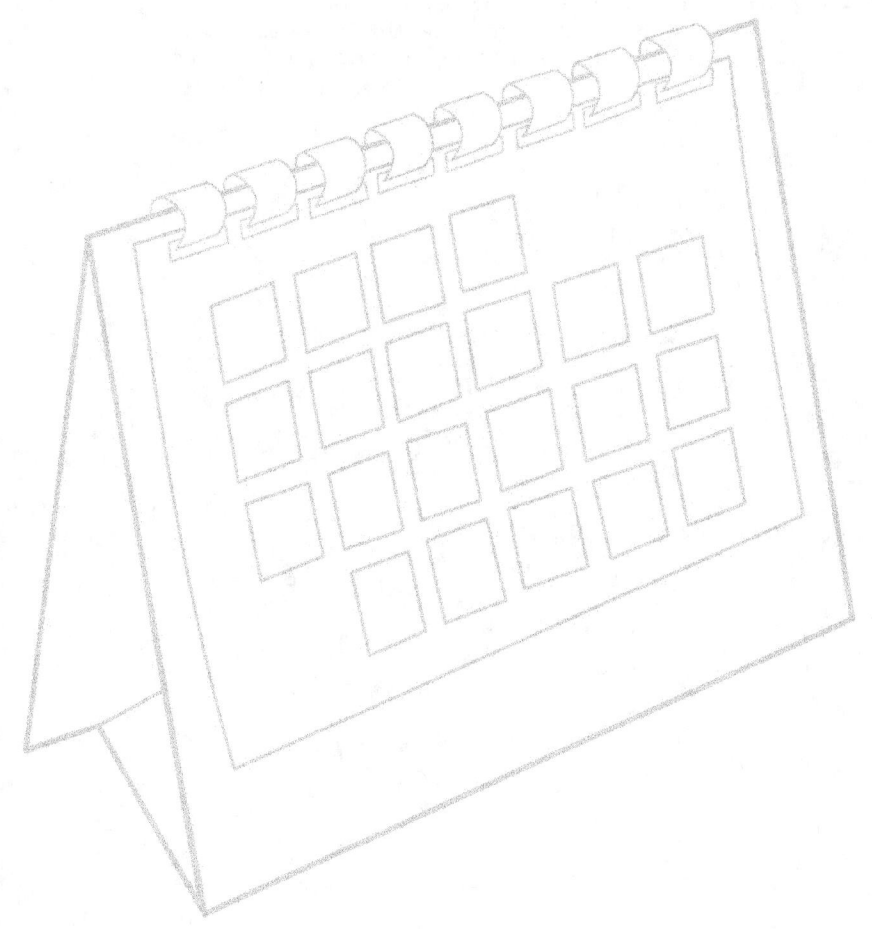

Date _____

Creativity - like human life itself - begins in darkness. -Julia Cameron

MORNING HABITS

What are the habits I want to build, increase or pay attention to? Sleep, water, meditation and journaling are the ones that are high on my list, what else do you want to add?

☐ 1. My time to get up is _____ am.
☐ 2. I will drink _____ glasses of water.
☐ 3. I did _____ minutes of Meditation.
☐ 4. I Journaled this morning.
☐ 5. _____
☐ 6. _____

Today's Creative Pursuit

What creativity will I pursue today? Baking, decorating, coloring, painting, music, creating software or a spreadsheet? The possibilities are endless.

_____
_____
_____

Today's Affirmations

Today's affirmations? I am creative, I am pursuing my dreams today, I am open to possibilities. What positive, present, personal statement are you making for yourself today? Repeat it at least 3 times today.

_____
_____
_____

One action I will take today to make myself or my life better.

Today I will try a new food, today I will go to the gym, today I will send that application, the possibilities are endless. What will you do today to make you life better?

_____
_____

One thing I will do today that is slightly out of my comfort zone.

Those scary things that you think you can't do. What is the worst that will happen? Make that phone call, ask for that raise, create that video, do what ever it takes to pull yourself out of your comfort zone, just one small thing each day will make a huge difference.

_____
_____

Doodle of the Day

Families are great murderers of the creative impulsive, particularly husbands.
-Brenda Ueland

How does this quote make you feel?

Notes

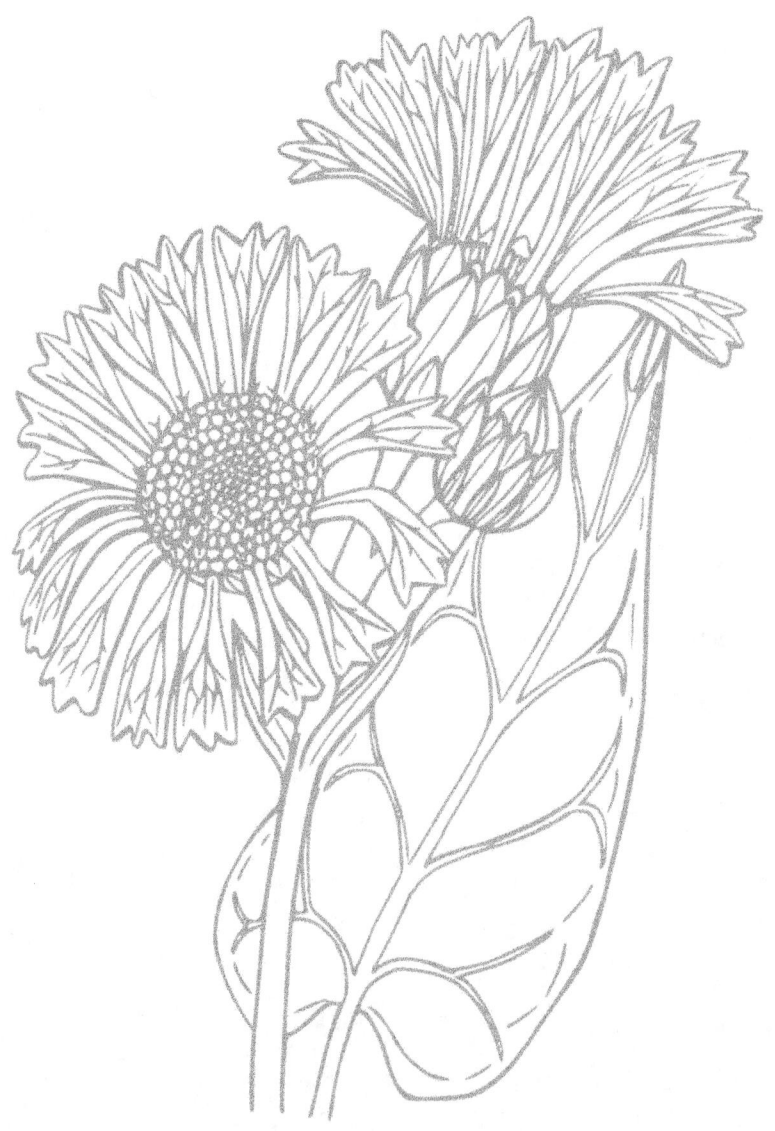

Date _____

> When we open ourselves to our creativity, we open ourselves to the creator's creativity within us and our lives.
> -Julia Cameron

MORNING HABITS

What are the habits I want to build, increase or pay attention to? Sleep, water , meditation and journaling are the ones that are high on my list, what else do you want to add?

- [ ] 1. My time to get up is _____ am.
- [ ] 2. I will drink _____ glasses of water.
- [ ] 3. I did _____ minutes of Meditation.
- [ ] 4. I Journaled this morning.
- [ ] 5. _____
- [ ] 6. _____

Today's Creative Pursuit

What creativity will I pursue today? Baking, decorating, coloring, painting, music, creating software or a spreadsheet? The possibilities are endless.

_____
_____

Today's Affirmations

Today's affirmations? I am creative, I am pursuing my dreams today, I am open to possibilities. What positive, present, personal statement are you making for yourself today? Repeat it at least 3 times today.

_____
_____

One action I will take today to make myself or my life better.

Today I will try a new food, today I will go to the gym, today I will send that application, the possibilities are endless. What will you do today to make you life better?

_____
_____

One thing I will do today that is slightly out of my comfort zone.

Those scary things that you think you can't do. What is the worst that will happen? Make that phone call, ask for that raise, create that video, do what ever it takes to pull yourself out of your comfort zone, just one small thing each day will make a huge difference.

_____
_____

Doodle of the Day

To think creatively, we must be able to look afresh at what we normally take for granted. -George Keller

How does this quote make you feel?

Notes

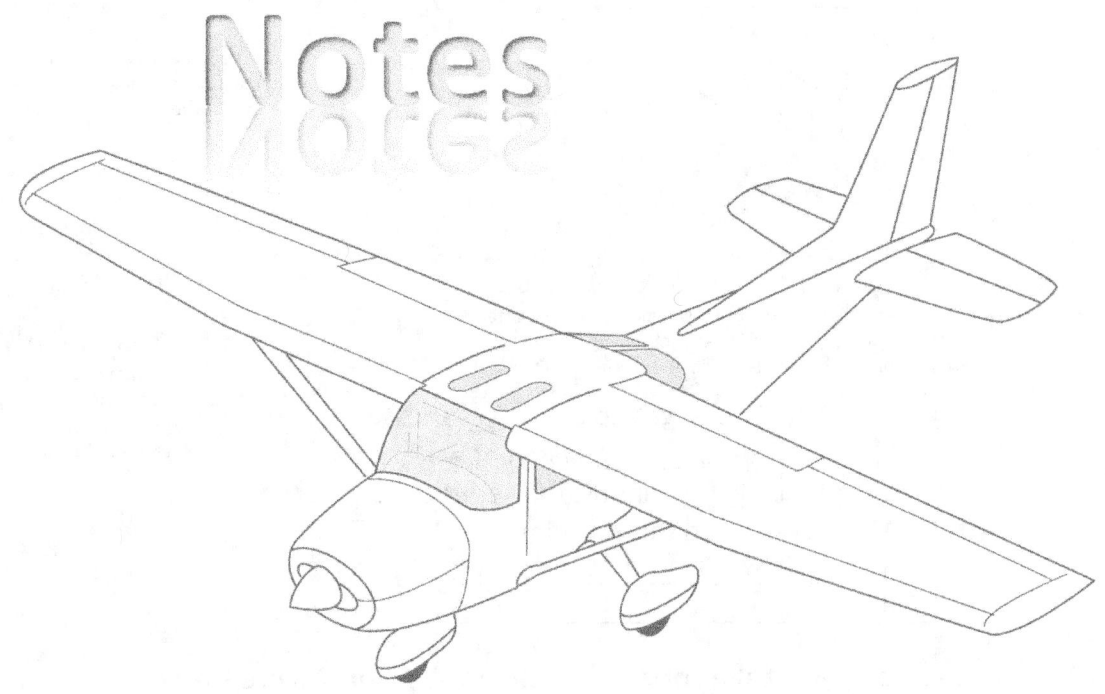

Date _____

> Imagination is not an icing on the cake of life but the oven in which it is baked.
> -Orna Ross

MORNING HABITS

What are the habits I want to build, increase or pay attention to? Sleep, water, meditation and journaling are the ones that are high on my list, what else do you want to add?

1. My time to get up is _____ am.
2. I will drink _____ glasses of water.
3. I did _____ minutes of Meditation.
4. I Journaled this morning.
5. _____
6. _____

Today's Creative Pursuit

What creativity will I pursue today? Baking, decorating, coloring, painting, music, creating software or a spreadsheet? The possibilities are endless.

_____
_____

Today's Affirmations

Today's affirmations? I am creative, I am pursuing my dreams today, I am open to possibilities. What positive, present, personal statement are you making for yourself today? Repeat it at least 3 times today.

_____
_____

One action I will take today to make myself or my life better.

Today I will try a new food, today I will go to the gym, today I will send that application, the possibilities are endless. What will you do today to make you life better?

_____
_____

One thing I will do today that is slightly out of my comfort zone.

Those scary things that you think you can't do. What is the worst that will happen? Make that phone call, ask for that raise, create that video, do what ever it takes to pull yourself out of your comfort zone, just one small thing each day will make a huge difference.

_____
_____

Doodle of the Day

Learn the craft of knowing how to open your heart and to turn on your creativity. There's a light inside of you. -Judith Jamison

How does this quote make you feel?

Notes

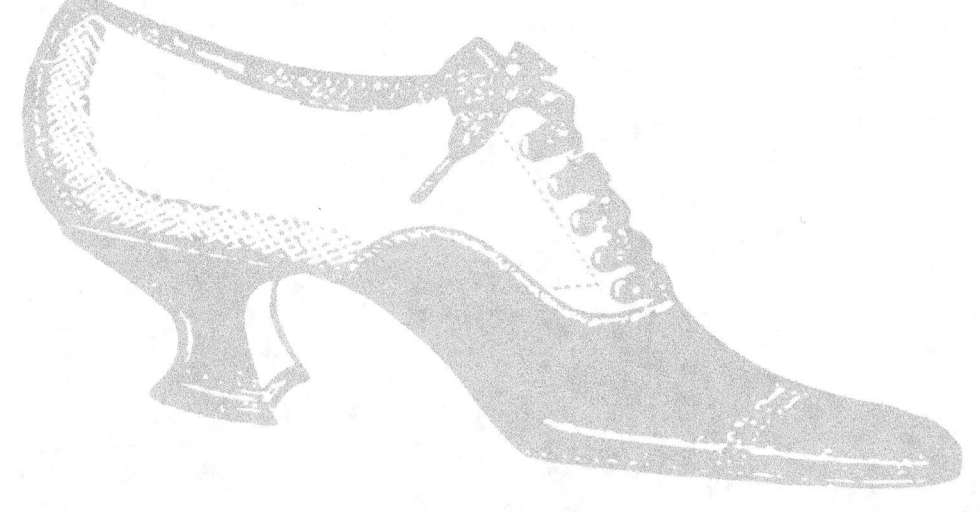

Date _____

Inspiration comes and goes; creativity is the result of practice. -Phil Cousineau

Today's Creative Pursuit

What creativity will I pursue today? Baking, decorating, coloring, painting, music, creating software or a spreadsheet? The possibilities are endless.

_____
_____
_____

MORNING HABITS

What are the habits I want to build, increase or pay attention to? Sleep, water, meditation and journaling are the ones that are high on my list, what else do you want to add?

1. My time to get up is _____ am.
2. I will drink _____ glasses of water.
3. I did _____ minutes of Meditation.
4. I Journaled this morning.
5. _____
6. _____

Today's Affirmations

Today's affirmations? I am creative, I am pursuing my dreams today, I am open to possibilities. What positive, present, personal statement are you making for yourself today? Repeat it at least 3 times today.

_____
_____
_____

One action I will take today to make myself or my life better.

Today I will try a new food, today I will go to the gym, today I will send that application, the possibilities are endless. What will you do today to make you life better?

_____
_____

One thing I will do today that is slightly out of my comfort zone.

Those scary things that you think you can't do. What is the worst that will happen? Make that phone call, ask for that raise, create that video, do what ever it takes to pull yourself out of your comfort zone, just one small thing each day will make a huge difference.

_____
_____

Doodle of the Day

Every artist has thousands of bad drawings in them and the only way to get rid of them is to draw them out. -Chuck Jones

How does this quote make you feel?

Notes

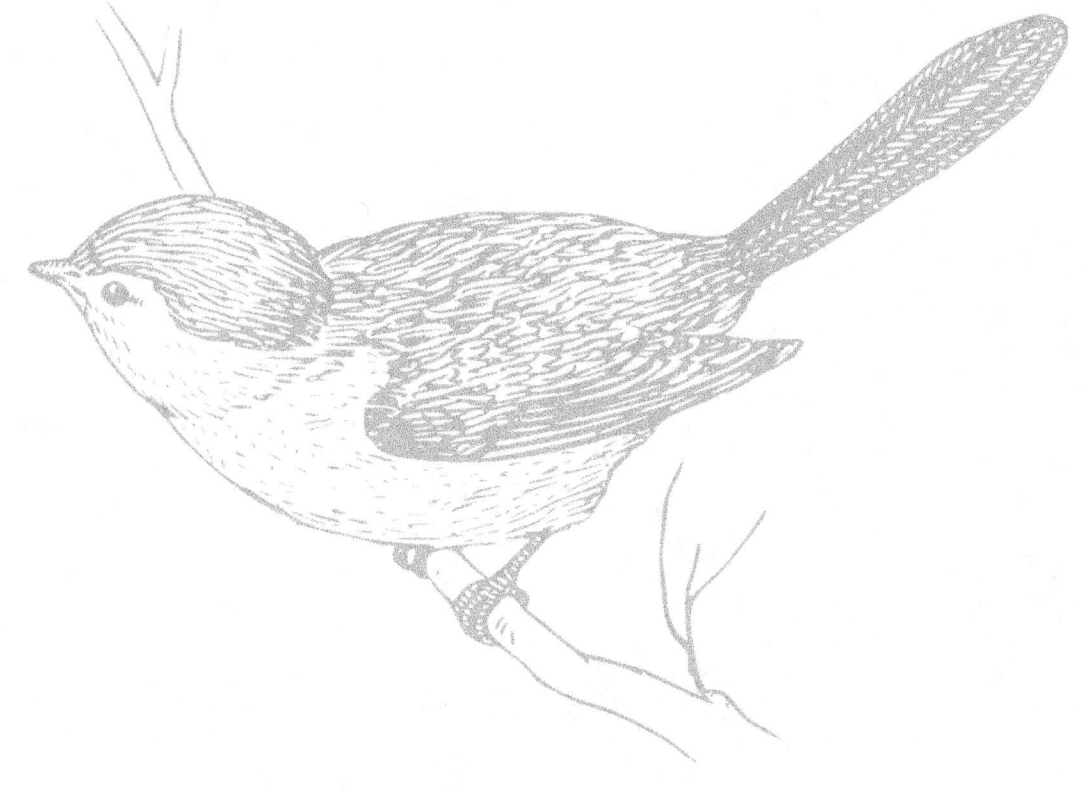

Date _____

> Creativity is fragile; if you don't nurture it, it can die, leaving you recycling old ideas and pretending they're fresh. It's a sure road to mediocrity. -Lee Silber

MORNING HABITS

What are the habits I want to build, increase or pay attention to? Sleep, water, meditation and journaling are the ones that are high on my list, what else do you want to add?

1. My time to get up is _____ am.
2. I will drink _____ glasses of water.
3. I did _____ minutes of Meditation.
4. I Journaled this morning.
5. _____
6. _____

Today's Creative Pursuit

What creativity will I pursue today? Baking, decorating, coloring, painting, music, creating software or a spreadsheet? The possibilities are endless.

_____
_____
_____

Today's Affirmations

Today's affirmations? I am creative, I am pursuing my dreams today, I am open to possibilities. What positive, present, personal statement are you making for yourself today? Repeat it at least 3 times today.

_____
_____
_____

One action I will take today to make myself or my life better.

Today I will try a new food, today I will go to the gym, today I will send that application, the possibilities are endless. What will you do today to make you life better?

_____
_____

One thing I will do today that is slightly out of my comfort zone.

Those scary things that you think you can't do. What is the worst that will happen? Make that phone call, ask for that raise, create that video, do what ever it takes to pull yourself out of your comfort zone, just one small thing each day will make a huge difference.

_____
_____

Doodle of the Day

Please DO waste art materials. Use paper. Empty paint jars. Deplete pens. if it's teaching you stuff, it's not being wasted. -Danny Gregory

How does this quote make you feel?

Notes

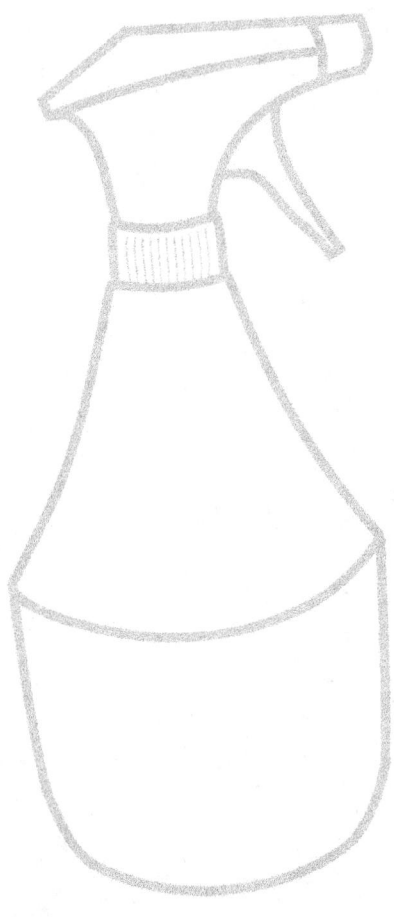

Date _____

> Creativity flows when the mind is light. Be light and ignite your imagination.
> -Amy Leigh Mercree

Today's Creative Pursuit

What creativity will I pursue today? Baking, decorating, coloring, painting, music, creating software or a spreadsheet? The possibilities are endless.

_____

_____

_____

MORNING HABITS

What are the habits I want to build, increase or pay attention to? Sleep, water, meditation and journaling are the ones that are high on my list, what else do you want to add?

- ☐ 1. My time to get up is _____ am.
- ☐ 2. I will drink _____ glasses of water.
- ☐ 3. I did _____ minutes of Meditation.
- ☐ 4. I Journaled this morning.
- ☐ 5. _____
- ☐ 6. _____

Today's Affirmations

Today's affirmations? I am creative, I am pursuing my dreams today, I am open to possibilities. What positive, present, personal statement are you making for yourself today? Repeat it at least 3 times today.

_____

_____

_____

One action I will take today to make myself or my life better.
Today I will try a new food, today I will go to the gym, today I will send that application, the possibilities are endless. What will you do today to make you life better?

_____

_____

One thing I will do today that is slightly out of my comfort zone.
Those scary things that you think you can't do. What is the worst that will happen? Make that phone call, ask for that raise, create that video, do what ever it takes to pull yourself out of your comfort zone, just one small thing each day will make a huge difference.

_____

_____

Doodle of the Day

Igniting your creative potentials opens you up to new learnings and insights.
-Deborah Day

How does this quote make you feel?

Notes

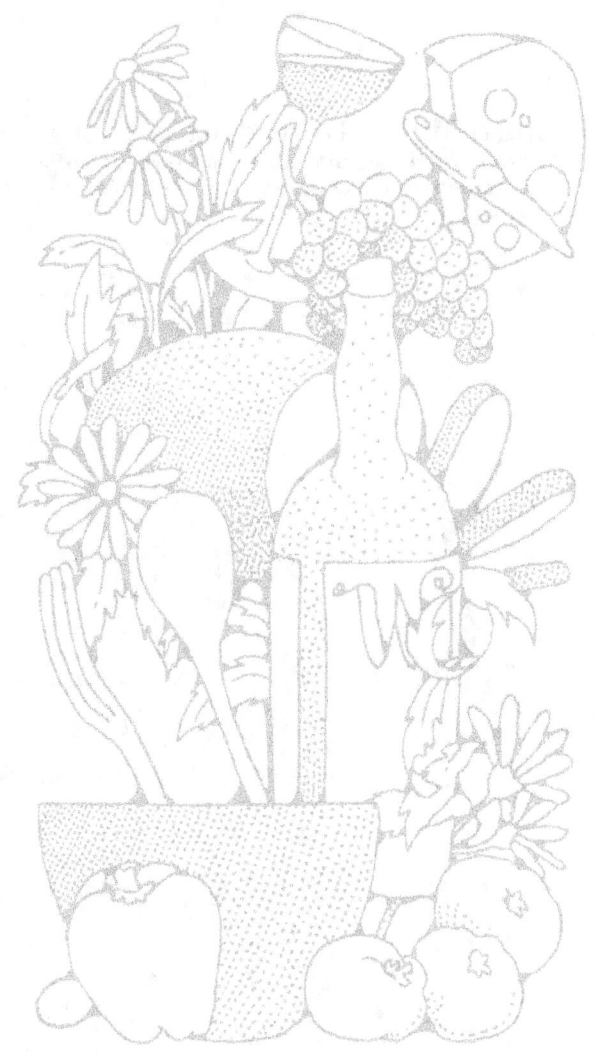

Date _____

Those who say there are no more original ideas need to get out of the way of those of us who are creating them.
-Steven Symes

MORNING HABITS

What are the habits I want to build, increase or pay attention to? Sleep, water, meditation and journaling are the ones that are high on my list, what else do you want to add?

☐ 1. My time to get up is _____ am.
☐ 2. I will drink _____ glasses of water.
☐ 3. I did _____ minutes of Meditation.
☐ 4. I Journaled this morning.
☐ 5. _____
☐ 6. _____

Today's Creative Pursuit

What creativity will I pursue today? Baking, decorating, coloring, painting, music, creating software or a spreadsheet? The possibilities are endless.

_____
_____
_____

Today's Affirmations

Today's affirmations? I am creative, I am pursuing my dreams today, I am open to possibilities. What positive, present, personal statement are you making for yourself today? Repeat it at least 3 times today.

_____
_____
_____

One action I will take today to make myself or my life better.

Today I will try a new food, today I will go to the gym, today I will send that application, the possibilities are endless. What will you do today to make you life better?

_____
_____

One thing I will do today that is slightly out of my comfort zone.

Those scary things that you think you can't do. What is the worst that will happen? Make that phone call, ask for that raise, create that video, do what ever it takes to pull yourself out of your comfort zone, just one small thing each day will make a huge difference.

_____
_____

Doodle of the Day

It's never too late to create! -Leena Ahmad Almashat

How does this quote make you feel?

Notes

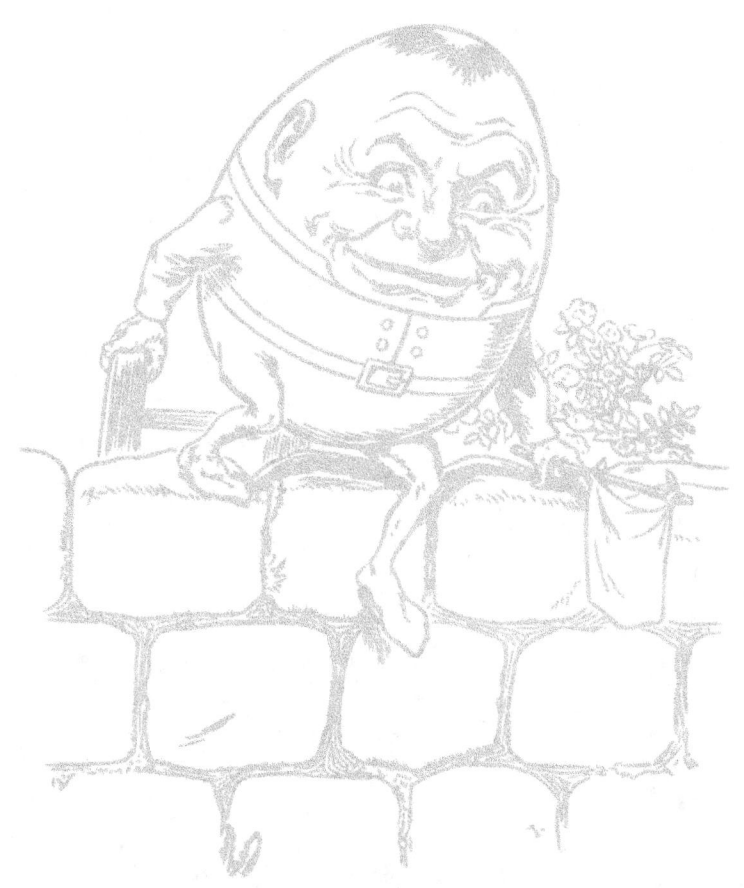

Date _____

> Playing is when you create the most.
> -Miguel Reynolds Brandao

MORNING HABITS

What are the habits I want to build, increase or pay attention to? Sleep, water, meditation and journaling are the ones that are high on my list, what else do you want to add?

- [ ] 1. My time to get up is _____ am.
- [ ] 2. I will drink _____ glasses of water.
- [ ] 3. I did _____ minutes of Meditation.
- [ ] 4. I Journaled this morning.
- [ ] 5. _____
- [ ] 6. _____

Today's Creative Pursuit

What creativity will I pursue today? Baking, decorating, coloring, painting, music, creating software or a spreadsheet? The possibilities are endless.

_____
_____
_____

Today's Affirmations

Today's affirmations? I am creative, I am pursuing my dreams today, I am open to possibilities. What positive, present, personal statement are you making for yourself today? Repeat it at least 3 times today.

_____
_____
_____

One action I will take today to make myself or my life better.

Today I will try a new food, today I will go to the gym, today I will send that application, the possibilities are endless. What will you do today to make you life better?

_____
_____

One thing I will do today that is slightly out of my comfort zone.

Those scary things that you think you can't do. What is the worst that will happen? Make that phone call, ask for that raise, create that video, do what ever it takes to pull yourself out of your comfort zone, just one small thing each day will make a huge difference.

_____
_____

Doodle of the Day

Inhale possibility, exhale creativity. -Laura Jaworski

How does this quote make you feel?

Notes

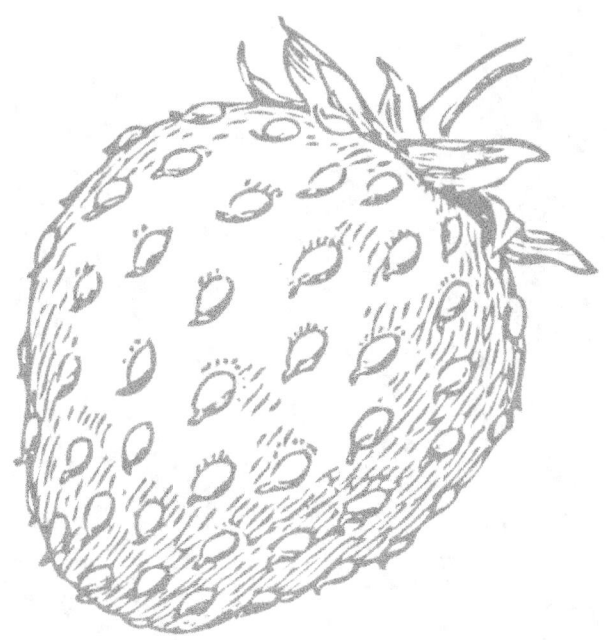

Date _____

Creativity is seeing things that other people can't. -Anthony T. Hincks

Today's Creative Pursuit

What creativity will I pursue today? Baking, decorating, coloring, painting, music, creating software or a spreadsheet? The possibilities are endless.

_____
_____
_____

MORNING HABITS

What are the habits I want to build, increase or pay attention to? Sleep, water, meditation and journaling are the ones that are high on my list, what else do you want to add?

- [ ] 1. My time to get up is _____ am.
- [ ] 2. I will drink _____ glasses of water.
- [ ] 3. I did _____ minutes of Meditation.
- [ ] 4. I Journaled this morning.
- [ ] 5. _____
- [ ] 6. _____

Today's Affirmations

Today's affirmations? I am creative, I am pursuing my dreams today, I am open to possibilities. What positive, present, personal statement are you making for yourself today? Repeat it at least 3 times today.

_____
_____
_____

One action I will take today to make myself or my life better.
Today I will try a new food, today I will go to the gym, today I will send that application, the possibilities are endless. What will you do today to make you life better?

_____
_____

One thing I will do today that is slightly out of my comfort zone.
Those scary things that you think you can't do. What is the worst that will happen? Make that phone call, ask for that raise, create that video, do what ever it takes to pull yourself out of your comfort zone, just one small thing each day will make a huge difference.

_____
_____

Doodle of the Day

Curiosity is straight fire for creativity. -Sam Harrison

How does this quote make you feel?

Notes

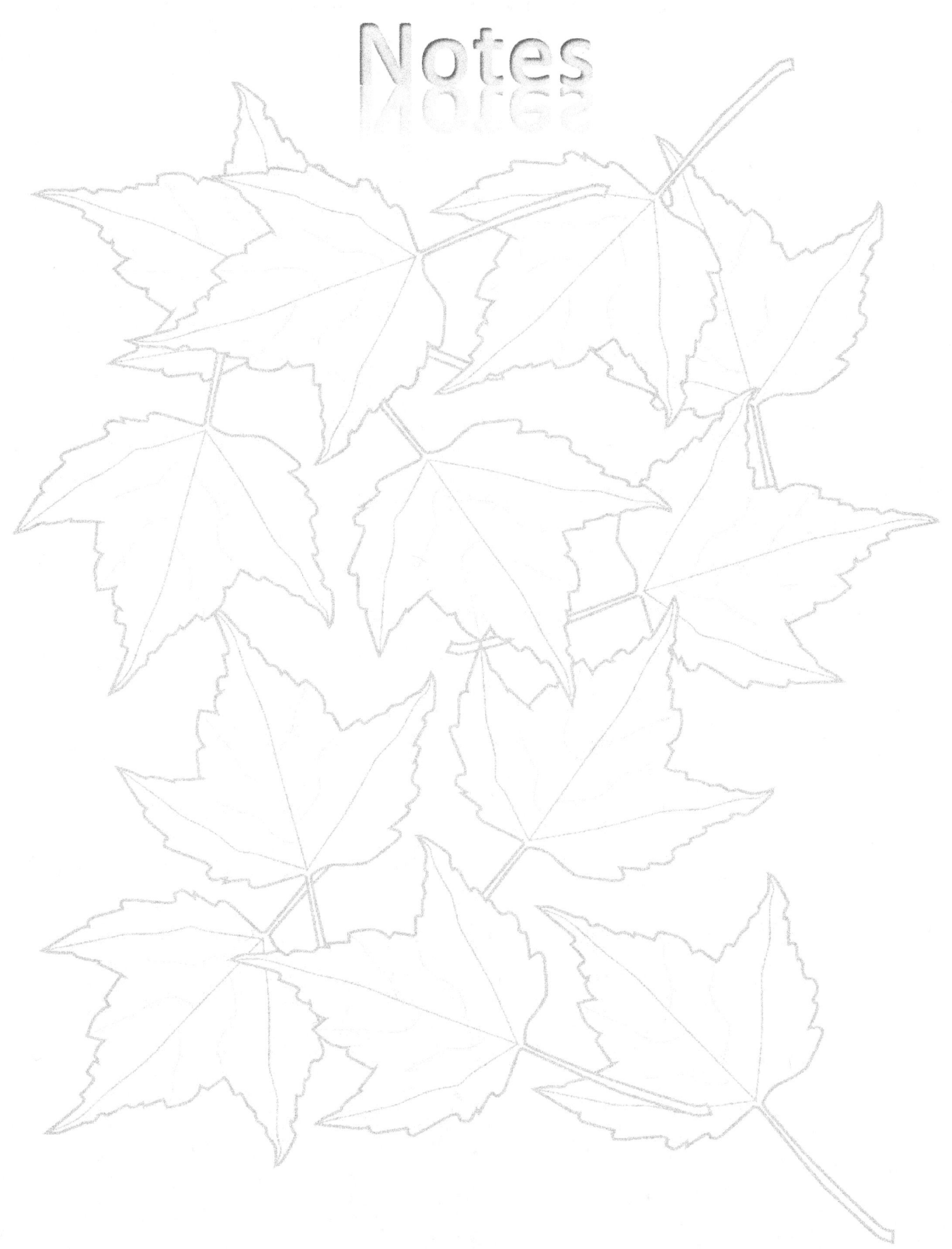

www.ingramcontent.com/pod-product-compliance
Lightning Source LLC
Chambersburg PA
CBHW082013230526
45466CB00021B/2263